One Place across Time

One Place across Time

Vancouver National Historic Reserve

Lois Mack

Introduction by William L. Lang

Vancouver National Historic Reserve Trust
Vancouver, Washington

© 2001   Vancouver National Historic Reserve Trust

750 Anderson Street

Vancouver, Washington, USA 98661

http://VancouverHistoricReserveTrust.org

Printed in the United States of America

Library of Congress Cataloging-in-Publication Data

Mack, Lois, 1947–

One place across time: Vancouver National Historic Reserve / by Lois Mack; introduction by William L. Lang.

     p. cm.

Companion guide to an exhibit held at the Visitor Center Museum, Vancouver National Historic Reserve.

Includes bibliographical references (p.) and index.

ISBN 0-9675250-1-2

1. Vancouver National Historic Reserve (Wash.)—Exhibitions. 2. Vancouver Region (Wash.)—History—Exhibitions. 3. Columbia River Region—History—Exhibitions. 4. Historic sites—Washington (State)—Vancouver Region—Exhibitions. I. Vancouver National Historic Reserve Trust. II Title.

F899.V2 .M27 1999

979.7'86–dc21   99-052240

CONTENTS

AN APPRECIATION

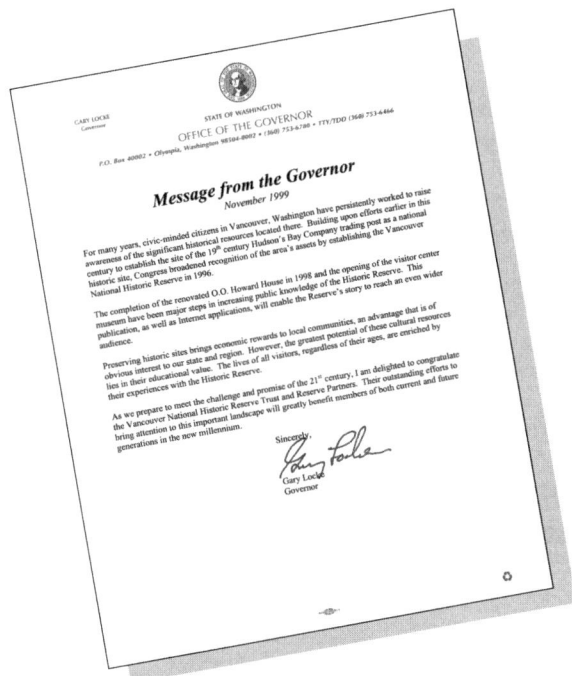

Message from the Governor

For many years, civic-minded citizens in Vancouver, Washington, have persistently worked to raise awareness of the significant historical resources located there. Building upon efforts earlier in this century to designate the site of the nineteenth-century Hudson's Bay Company trading post as a national historic site, Congress broadened recognition of the area's assets by establishing the Vancouver National Historic Reserve in 1996.

The completion of the renovated O.O. Howard House in 1998 and the opening of the Visitor Center Museum have been major steps in increasing public knowledge of the historic reserve. This publication, as well as Internet applications, will allow the reserve's story to reach an even wider audience.

Preserving historic sites brings economic rewards to local communities, an advantage that is of obvious interest to our state and region. However, the greatest potential of these cultural resources lies in their educational value. The lives of all visitors, regardless of age, are enriched by their experiences with the Vancouver National Historic Reserve and its programs.

As we prepare to meet the challenge and promise of the twenty-first century, I am delighted to congratulate the Vancouver National Historic Reserve Trust and its partners. Their outstanding efforts to bring attention to this important landscape will greatly benefit members of both current and future generations in the new millennium.

Sincerely,
Gary Locke
Governor of Washington

FOREWORD

Time is one measure by which we evaluate our existence. In the world of our daily lives, we often use time simply to plan our day, or to enclose the brief memory of a recent event. But sometimes we take a finer measurement. Our thoughts assume a deeper reflection of past events and their significance in our lives. We look at our actions for what they will mean to a world yet born.

Such thought and action are reflected in the permanent exhibit at the General O.O. Howard House and in the broad cultural landscape of the Vancouver National Historic Reserve. Here, tangible evidence of our human history has been preserved because of the past and current actions of people who have taken a finer measurement.

Public and private partnership efforts have led Congress, over the past fifty years, to protect by legislation this place and its history, to leave it "unimpaired for the enjoyment of future generations," in the language of the National Park Service. Through the preservation of cultural landscapes such as this one, and through the artifacts and interpretations of the "One Place across Time" exhibit, these future generations will be able to reflect meaningfully on a small part of human existence.

Just as the landscape is more than a collection of buildings and vistas, the exhibit is more than a simple array of objects and words. Both provide us with the means to make connections between the past and the present, to reflect on the lives and stories of people who once occupied these buildings and walked these grounds, and on those who will do so hence.

To borrow from the late Freeman Tilden, writing on the subject of interpretation in the national parks, cultural landscapes and human objects represent the lives and acts of people. We are those people, along with our past and future generations.

In our continuing efforts to give a broader voice to the human stories of our existence, the preservation of places of significance in our nation's history—both natural and cultural—must be coupled with the ability to share these stories with all people. Through the dissemination of information in exhibits and publications such as this one, and through other means such as the Internet, we can now begin to reach the broader audience that Congress envisioned when it established a *national* reserve in Vancouver. The National Park Service, with more than 370 national park sites across this nation, feels at home with the efforts and successes in Vancouver, and is pleased to be a partner in the "One Place across Time" exhibit and the Vancouver National Historic Reserve.

Tony Sisto, superintendent, 1995–2000
Fort Vancouver National Historic Site

PREFACE

The establishment of the Vancouver National Historic Reserve in 1996 marked a watershed in the community's efforts to preserve, interpret, and enhance historic assets in Vancouver. It created a partnership among public agencies, established a common management plan, and provided a vision for enhancement of the historic reserve for public benefit.

In 1998, the One Place across Time Committee, previously comprised of private citizens, became the Vancouver National Historic Reserve Trust, a nonprofit educational organization. The reserve trust carries on the strong tradition of community support through advocacy, public-private partnerships, and fund raising. The diligence, commitment, and perseverance of volunteers and professionals have energized activity in the historic reserve, resulting in such projects as the renovation of the O.O. Howard House, the establishment of the Murdock Aviation Center, the installation of the permanent "One Place across Time" museum exhibit, and the publication of *One Place across Time: Vancouver National Historic Reserve*.

Today, the Vancouver National Historic Reserve Trust continues to bring definition and focus to earlier community involvement, and a collective effort of stewardship has been forged with the city of Vancouver, the National Park Service, the U.S. Army, and the state of Washington. The reserve trust gives voice to the private sector, allowing citizens to participate and work together with public agencies to preserve a historical learning center for future generations, and thereby to enrich our lives.

Bruce Hagensen and Ed Lynch, co-presidents
Board of Trustees, Vancouver National Historic Reserve Trust

ACKNOWLEDGMENTS

This exhibit project and book are the result of the contributions of many people over a number of years. First, I would like to acknowledge the assistance of John Marshall, executive director of the Vancouver National Historic Reserve Trust, who gave initial approval for this publication and offered valuable insights along the way. John Marshall's leadership and dedication to the vision of the Vancouver National Historic Reserve as a public resource is an example worthy of emulation. His contribution is especially admirable in that he has served in a full-time voluntary capacity.

I would like to thank the following individuals for their thoughtful critical comments and participation in the development of the written material: David Hansen, curator and historian at Fort Vancouver National Historic Site; Bill Lang, director of the Center for Columbia River History; LTC Robert Knight, commander, Vancouver Barracks; Tony Sisto, superintendent of Fort Vancouver National Historic Site; Jennifer Mack, journalist, San Francisco; Steve McGeorge, director of the Oregon Military Museum; Charlene Dahlen, Reserve Trust development director; Garry Breckon, former museum director, Oregon Historical Society; Albert Wooldridge, Battleground, Washington; National Park Service interpreters at the Gen. O.O. Howard House; David Freece, director, Cowlitz County Historical Society; the helpful staffs of the Oregon Historical Society, Washington State Historical Society, and Clark County Museum; and the many contributors to the exhibition listed on the following pages.

Credit is also due Larry Rank, who transformed words and images into a cohesive book design and handled all technical aspects of prepress and printing. His patience is extraordinary. Jesse Champlin, of New York City, photographed all the artifacts on one of his trips to Oregon in 1999. Debra Semrau, Reserve Trust curator, assisted with production details. Rick Harmon, former editor of the *Oregon Historical Quarterly*, helped with the final copy editing. I apologize to anyone I have inadvertently left out.

Production of this publication was assisted by an appropriation obtained through the Department of the Interior, National Park Service.

Finally, I would like to thank Doug Magedanz for his invaluable assistance, astute comments, and critical perspective from the beginning.

EXHIBITION CONTRIBUTORS

The Vancouver National Historic Reserve Trust created this exhibition in cooperation with the National Park Service, U.S. Army, city of Vancouver, and state of Washington. The exhibit was made possible by financial support from the M.J. Murdock Charitable Trust and the National Park Service. The Reserve Trust Board of Trustees wishes to thank the following organizations and individuals for their invaluable contributions.

Exhibit Team

Executive Director
John Marshall, Vancouver National
    Historic Reserve Trust

Exhibit Project Manager, Education Director
Lois Mack, Vancouver National Historic
    Reserve Trust

Design and Fabrication Manager
Shab Levy

Exhibit Designer
Gary Larsen

Graphic Designer
Larry Rank

Exhibit Engineer
Forrest Zuercher

Contributors/Lenders

Center for Columbia River History
Clark County Museum
Clark/Vancouver Television
Columbia Basin Basketry Guild,
    Curatorial Committee
Fort Vancouver National
    Historic Site
Gifford Pinchot National Forest
Howard University
Hudson's Bay Company Archives,
    Winnipeg, Manitoba
Lelooska Foundation,
    Ariel, Washington
Library of Congress, American
    Folklife Center
Minnesota Historical Society
Nez Perce Music Archive,
    Washington State University
Oregon Historical Society
Oregon Military Museum,
    Clackamas, Oregon
Oregon Museum of Science
    & Industry
University of Washington
Vancouver Barracks Retiree
    Sub-Council
Vancouver Maritime Museum,
    Vancouver, British Columbia
Vancouver National Historic
    Reserve Trust
Washington State Historical Society
Washington State University

Penny Baz
Garry Breckon
Warren Castrey
Bob Chase
Jim Delgado
Dale Denny
Christine Donaugh
Bill Farr
Ann Goodhart
Eugene Hunn
Sam Jones
Randy Kau'i
Paul Lawson
Louis Lee
Rick MacHale
Jeffrey Mack
Jennifer Mack
Doug Magedanz
Kay Milberger
Bill Moore
Pearl Morrison
Sherry Mowatt
Hudson Paddock
Norris Perkins
Jim Raley
Helen Sareen
Caroline Stanek
Bob Twyman
Ted Van Arsdol
Suzy Vincent
Jason Wulf
Henry Zenk

Photographic Credits

Academy of Natural Sciences of
    Philadelphia
American Antiquarian Society,
    Worcester, Massachusetts
Beinecke Library, Yale University,
    New Haven, Connecticut
Boston Public Library
Clark County Museum
Dale Denny
Fort Vancouver National
    Historic Site
Gifford Pinchot National Forest
Howard House Collection
Hudson's Bay Company Archives
John Clymer Museum,
    Ellensburg, Washington
Kaiser Permanente
Kansas State Historical Society
Louis Lee
Missouri Historical Society
National Archives
National Gallery of Canada
National Maritime Museum,
    Greenwich, England
Oregon Historical Society
The *Oregonian*
Peabody & Essex Museum,
    Salem, Massachusetts
Pearson Field Historical Society
Private Collection
Public Archives of Canada, Ottawa
Royal Engineers Library,
    Kent, England
Royal Ontario Museum, Toronto
Stark Museum of Art, Orange, Texas
U.S. Army
U.S. Naval Academy Museum,
    Annapolis, Maryland
Washington State Historical Society

INTRODUCTION

HISTORY IN THIS PLACE ∾ Historians are ever mindful of dates and what people have done. Regardless of the subjects they pursue, they have a singular curiosity about change over time. They focus on the actors, the events, and the ideas that held sway, and they take special note of the places where things happened. It can be a tedious business, tracking down great and small occurrences, but the hope is that making sense of the past helps us to understand the differences between today and yesterday.

A crucial aid in this study is establishing something historians call historical context. It is an uninspiring phrase, but it stands for the most intriguing part of our investigations of the past. Historical context is setting. It is the larger environment connected to people, actions, ideas, and places. It is the complex set of relationships that tie individuals to groups, places to region, and one time to another.

The Vancouver National Historic Reserve is alive with historical context, and without it the place would make little sense. A walk down Evergreen Boulevard along Officers Row makes the point. The buildings, their arrangement, and the setting clearly exude another time. People lived and worked here a century ago; yet this is a community existing at the beginning of the twenty-first century, complete with car and bus traffic on the road and international air traffic overhead. The buildings mix old and new. They are renovations, with attention paid to important historical details for authenticity and to modern technologies for efficiency. Officers Row is a preserved landscape, and its rationale is history. But what is the content of that history? How can we make sense of it? What does it tell us about our past?

Officers Row served a military purpose, as the commemorative plaques along the sidewalk make evident. The plaques honor men who served at Vancouver Barracks, some with familiar names, some not so familiar: U.S. Grant, Phil Sheridan, George McClellan, from the Civil War era; Oliver Otis Howard, from the Indian war period; George C. Marshall, from the 1930s. They share little beyond their service in the military, and that they spent time at this place, the first regular army post in the Pacific Northwest. We know their names because of their exploits on battlefields far from this corner of the nation, and it is that recognition that attracts our attention and surprise.

U.S. Grant, victor at Appomattox and president, lived at Vancouver. George C. Marshall, World War II five-star general, great secretary of state, and author of the Marshall Plan, spent time here. This is where historical context helps. Grant, Sheridan, McClellan, and Marshall served at Vancouver Barracks before they became heroic, before they won celebrity status. Their lives at Vancouver might have presaged their later successes, but the reverse is more likely. What they did later enhances their Vancouver experiences. When we invoke their names, we borrow their celebrity to bestow additional history on this landscape. Officers Row gains credibility and stature because they lived here, regardless of what they may have done while they lived here.

For our understanding of Officers Row, what these nascent generals did at Vancouver is more important than their later exploits. And what they did here turns out to be what we might expect. They performed their duties well, maybe even exceptionally. U.S. Grant, for example, worked as a quartermaster during the early 1850s, when the U.S. Army spent much of its energy at Vancouver assisting agricultural and commercial settlement in the area. The generous homestead opportunities in Oregon during the 1840s and 1850s beckoned thousands to make claims in the region on lands that were still in Native hands and not yet surveyed completely. Grant's job entailed purchasing and maintaining a stock of goods for the garrisoned soldiers. He was part of an occupational force that meant to guarantee a domesticated frontier for newly settled agriculturalists.

In 1877, twenty-four years after Grant left Vancouver and three years into Oliver Otis Howard's tenure as commander here, the landscape had dramatically changed. Land-hungry settlers in the Northwest had fomented conflicts with Indians who objected to their treatment by the federal government. It fell to O.O. Howard to enforce the government's will against a recalcitrant population of Nez Perce in northeastern Oregon. Sometimes at a pace considered dilatory by his superiors, Howard dogged a group of 800 men, women, and children who shunned conflict for four months over 1,300 miles of terrain, finally to force their surrender on a snow-dusted battlefield in northern Montana.

The historical context of Grant's experience and Howard's differs in almost every imaginable way. In 1853, the military compound included a headquarters building and several outbuildings. No improved roads led anywhere from Vancouver. Steamboats had begun service in Portland only two years before. By 1880, Howard's residence—today's O.O. Howard House—had been completed, but the residences that make up what we call Officers Row had yet to be built, and the sidewalk was added only after the turn of the century. No railroads served Vancouver. Packet ships from Portland and Astoria brought goods and ferried people on the Willamette and Columbia rivers. A few rustic military roads connected Vancouver with Monticello (site of modern Longview), Chehalis, Olympia, and Puget Sound.

The relationships between the officers and their missions, between the military encampment and its immediate surroundings, and between this stretch of riverside landscape and the rest of the Northwest highlight the most obvious differences in historical context. The more we know about these contexts the better we can understand how and why this landscape is historic.

How this place became historic is also a matter of context, with explanations that include happenstance and the consequences of national policies. Established by Congress in 1996, the Vancouver National Historic Reserve extends over 366 acres on the north bank of the Columbia River, east of downtown Vancouver, Washington. Much of this landscape is open, with a minimum of development and an unusual percentage of historically protected space. Its existence, preserved as it is from twenty-first-century disturbance, makes Vancouver unique among cities in the Northwest.

More important, the acreage is the site of one of the region's first major non-Indian settlements, headquarters for a vast commercial trading firm in the mid-nineteenth century; the site of the Northwest's first permanent military establishment; and the location of military industries during two world wars in the twentieth century. Even more remarkable, because the place belonged to the British-chartered Hudson's Bay Company (HBC) for a quarter century and later became the property of federal, state, and city governments, private development has generally been kept beyond its perimeter.

This is a landscape preserved by historical context, by the succession of its claimants, and by the services it has rendered the region's residents. Power directed outward from this place affected every group in the region, from the trade relationships conducted by the Hudson's Bay Company to the military missions and materiel sent forth from here. The activities that took place here reflect the culture's major purpose—settlement and development of the region. Preservation of the Vancouver National Historic Reserve also ensures the preservation of memories, documents, and objects of material culture that shed light on what happened here or had its genesis here.

With that purpose in mind, local people began a preservation effort at the beginning of the twentieth century. Citizens urged Congress to establish a historic monument to commemorate the site of the Hudson's Bay Company post, Fort Vancouver. Congress responded by authorizing archaeological and historical investigations, and by 1966 the National Park Service had begun the first reconstructions on the old fur post's site.

Three decades later, Congress revisited the importance of this landscape when it created a special commission to study how this historic space, in the heart of a major metropolitan area, should be managed. Two years of study and discussion confirmed that important things happened here, and that the legacies of those events and the people who lived here have relevance to our lives. The studies concluded that the entire area needed protection, that it should be a place of public education, and that the public would gain from knowing more about Vancouver's past.

3

WHAT PEOPLE DID HERE ∽ This landscape, as with all others on the globe, bears the evidence of earlier human activities. Sometimes that evidence is veiled or hidden from view. The imprint of earlier events is not always apparent. Two examples from this landscape make the point: the shipways on the Columbia River at the Kaiser shipyard site, from the twentieth century; and the artifacts of the fur trade buried beneath the stockade grounds at Fort Vancouver, remnants of the nineteenth century.

The shipways are veiled. Although they can be seen readily by boat from the river, they are partially hidden amid the commercial buildings in the Columbia Business Park, south of State Route 14 and the railroad berm. You can see them clearly from an observatory tower at Marine Park, but it takes some imagination to envision the incredible activity that took place there between 1942 and 1945. During those years, tens of thousands of workers built more than 140 warships and sent them down the shipways to the Columbia and then to war service. The Kaiser yards were efficient. Men and women in that three-shift environment made industrial history, leaving behind the skeletal shipways as evidence.

The evidence of activities from a much earlier era, however, is completely out of sight. Archaeologists have probed, dug, and sifted the ground on the site of the Hudson's Bay Company's Fort Vancouver and retrieved more than a million artifacts that document another kind of hectic activity. The ceramics, lithics, bottle glass, tobacco pipes, iron implements, glass beads, military objects, and dozens of other kinds of items unearthed from the extensive plain just north of State Route 14 make the work and living that took place at Fort Vancouver between 1829 and 1860 tangible. The National Park Service collection of these artifacts in the reconstructed fur warehouse lets us do more than imagine the substance of that distant era—we can touch it and ask questions. The things discarded and left to be buried by time mark a quarter-century of work that paced itself on a seasonal calendar determined by the needs of fur trapping and agricultural operations. The artifacts are evidence of people-to-people exchanges and the equipment that facilitated it all.

The chronological and cultural distance between the shipways on the Columbia and HBC artifacts dug up from the old stockade grounds and the village is considerable and instructive. There is little in common between the fur post and the shipyards. While their historical contexts clash in comparisons of technologies, concentration of activity, and purposes, they left their marks on this same landscape. They share a connection with this place, but the links between them are often indirect, even accidental.

HBC's quarter-century here on an accessible and well-developed landscape established a perfect foundation for the frontier U.S. Army, where roads, broad fields, and the nearness of the Columbia served the military's needs. The army's nineteenth-century garrisons led seamlessly to the twentieth century and its aviation and military industries of World War I and World War II. The more important connection between the HBC and Kaiser eras, however, is in the consequences of what people did here. What they did made a difference to this region and the larger world. It is that activity—at least in part—that the Vancouver National Historic Reserve commemorates. But to understand what happened here, we need to keep historical context in mind.

Native people had used this landscape for hundreds of years before Gov. George Simpson selected Jolie Prairie for a new HBC fur post in 1824. Indians used the place to gather food, as a temporary residence, and as access to the Columbia. The HBC took hold of the land as an instrument of a larger design. The people who worked here, from Chief Factor John McLoughlin to the day laborers at the fort, focused on the business of trade, the exchange of natural resources from the region for monetary wealth. And the region they tapped from this fort location extended from present-day northern California to southeastern Alaska, and as far east as the crest of the Rockies in Montana, Idaho, and British Columbia. A funnel-like labyrinth of river and overland transportation linked more than thirty-five fur outposts in the region to Fort Vancouver. Small groups of fur gleaners—the so-called brigades—fanned out from Fort Vancouver year after year, returning with furs worth thousands of pounds sterling.

It was all about money and the profits these activities brought to HBC stockholders in England. The men working here forged tools in the smithy, cared for livestock, or conducted trade with Indians to the benefit of men unseen and an ocean away. The consequence was the creation of a trading empire that changed the face of the Northwest forever.

The Hudson's Bay Company's mercantile landscape contrasts starkly with Henry J. Kaiser's war-industry domain at Vancouver. Raw materials from near and far were transformed here into the vectors and implements of war. The yards produced Liberty Ships, Baby Flat Tops, and LSTs that battled against Axis navies. Unlike HBC's fur post, which brought the world to the Columbia, the shipyards sent the products of the Columbia to a world at war.

Along the Columbia, the shipyard stood midway between the region's first aluminum plant and Bonneville Dam, making it part of a significantly larger industrial place. It was a massively altered landscape, where engineering had fundamentally changed the Columbia and created a new world of opportunities for work and industry. In that new environment, men and women labored here for their country and for good wages. They focused enormous energy and ingenuity on a narrow purpose and achieved great feats. Working in mammoth welding and fabrication shops, they built ships in record time—in three days they could produce an LST (Landing Ship Tank). Those ships helped change history's direction for the second half of the twentieth century.

Events and developments that change the direction of history deserve notice. It can be argued that the HBC's creation of a new natural-resource economy in the Pacific Northwest during the first half of the nineteenth century canted the future of this region as much as the Allied victory in World War II spun the world differently. But smaller events and episodes can also make a difference and lend importance to place. The presence of African Americans in the frontier army, for example, emphasizes the point that ethnic diversity was endemic in the post–Civil War military. The Ninth and Tenth Cavalry, the so-called Buffalo Soldiers, originated during the Civil War in Kansas, but they gained fame on the frontier, where they served with great distinction until 1900. The army garrisoned them throughout the West, including at Vancouver Barracks, and assigned them to duties ranging from battles against Indians to patrols at industrial labor disputes. First Sgt. Moses Williams, a Medal of Honor holder, served in the Ninth Cavalry and at Vancouver Barracks as an ordnance sergeant. He is buried at the Post Cemetery.

The unjustified imprisonment of more than thirty Nez Perce at Vancouver Barracks in 1877–1878 is another reminder of the role this place played in the lives of non-European people in the Northwest. As hostilities flared on the Nez Perce Indian Reservation in Idaho in 1877, a military detachment captured Red Heart's band and roughly packed them off, as threats to the peace, to Vancouver Barracks for detention. General Howard's troops hastily constructed a corral south of the parade grounds to keep and contain Red Heart's families. Although the group included at least seventeen women and children—hardly a war party—the military authorities held them hostage to the war effort for eight months.

The incident is best understood as an episode in the larger campaign by military authorities in the Northwest to dominate Native people. This often meant the selective enforcement of treaty provisions. For many Indians in the Northwest, Vancouver Barracks stood as a symbol of an alien government's power and determination to control their lives. It's a role better commemorated than celebrated, and one that must be understood and not forgotten.

Some events, however, are celebrations in themselves. A few become icons, events that stand as characterizations of the place. Two at Vancouver Barracks that fall into this category highlight the role aviation has played here in the twentieth century. The broad prairie that had attracted HBC managers in the 1820s drew attention from early fliers nearly a century later. From the 1910s through the interwar years, the grassy plain south of the parade grounds became a favored flying strip for local aviators.

Among them was Silas Christofferson, a self-taught airplane builder who launched his bamboo-framed plane from the roof of the newly built Multnomah Hotel in Portland on June 12, 1912, for a spectacular flight to Vancouver Barracks. A publicity event, Christofferson's hop across the Columbia was a harbinger of two decades of barnstorming aviation at the airfield, which gained the title Pearson Field in 1925, in honor of Alex Pearson, a local flier and Army Air Corps pilot who died testing high-speed planes in 1924.

A second aviation event topped Christofferson's achievement in world-class fashion. In June 1937, three Russian aviators completed the world's first nonstop transpolar flight when they touched down at Pearson Field. Their ANT-25, a single-engine plane with a 112-foot wingspan, looked more like a glider than a propeller plane, and like no other at the field. The ANT-25's crew—Valeri Chkalov, Georgiy Baidukov, and Alexander Belyakov—became Russian and Vancouver heroes simultaneously, and thereby thrust little Pearson Field into the international spotlight. Nothing quite as spectacular in aeronautics has happened in the region since that day in 1937.

HOW THEY LIVED ON THIS HISTORIC LANDSCAPE

Walking these grounds amid structures that represent more than 150 years of historical events, we can lose sight of the truism that people make history. Piecing together a record of their lives is part sleuthing and part imagining. The thoughts of Red Heart's people behind the fifteen-foot-high stockade walls in 1877, for example, are beyond our immediate reach, but through family oral narratives we can retrieve a sense of their experience. The daily work of soldiers, from the pre–Civil War era to readying hospital supplies for the 1991 Gulf War, are in the documentary record, as are much of the details of frontier military excursions, the work of the "Spruce Soldiers" during World War I, and the activities of Army Air Corps squadrons. But in order to re-create the texture of life in earlier eras, we need to understand the social conditions here. It requires another foray into historical context.

Because this landscape has been the domain of corporate and government entities, nearly everyone who came and spent time here belonged to an identifiable group. They lived and worked in a world full of rules, prerogatives, and specific social order. Society here during the 1840s, for example, ordered itself by class, race, and work. The Hudson's Bay Company lived by hierarchy. The Governor and Committee in London—the stockholders—stood at the top of the social-mercantile pyramid. In

North America, Gov. George Simpson oversaw all operations, and at Fort Vancouver, Chief Factor Dr. John McLoughlin carried full authority to effect policies and manage affairs, business and social, throughout the Columbia Department.

McLoughlin was arguably one of the most powerfully placed individuals in the entire history of the Pacific Northwest, for his authority extended over hundreds of thousands of square miles and affected thousands of Natives and hundreds of HBC men. He directed more than 600 non-Native employees, who included well-defined ranks of traders, clerks, interpreters, tradesmen, apprentices, and laborers. The HBC employed Indians as laborers and brought Native Hawaiians—Kanakas—to Vancouver as sawmill and agricultural workers. Residences, segregation of activities, and even dining arrangements reflected the company's focus on social class.

Visitors to Fort Vancouver noted its peculiar organization, but more often they marveled at its surprising sophistication. Narcissa Whitman called it the "New York of the Pacific Ocean" in 1836, when she and Marcus Whitman stayed as McLoughlin's guests. As a supply depot and travelers' rest, Fort Vancouver became a staging point for a broad range of visitors. They included: naturalists David Douglas, John Scouler, and John K. Townsend; explorers Charles Wilkes and John Charles Fremont; missionaries Jason Lee and Francis Norbert Blanchet;

interlopers, such as Nathaniel Wyeth; spies, such as Henry J. Warre and Mervin Vavasour; and a long list of Oregon pioneers who made Fort Vancouver a stop on their trek to the Willamette Valley. They came to this place en route to someplace else, and with purposes quite apart from fur trading.

For David Douglas, Fort Vancouver introduced him to a wondrous world of new flora and served as an outfitting point for his historic botanical surveys. For Jason Lee and the Whitmans, Vancouver became a lifeline for their devoted but unsuccessful efforts to convert Indian people to new religious belief. During the second quarter of the nineteenth century, Vancouver was a landscape common to widely dispersed social, economic, and political activities in the region.

During the twentieth century, the orientation and spectrum of people drawn here changed dramatically. Military purpose, especially during World War I and World War II, yanked men and women out of their lives and sent them here from all regions of the nation. In 1917 and 1918, they came as nurses, new recruits, spruce mill workers, line officers, and soldiers to transform Vancouver Barracks into a weapon to help win the "war to end all wars." Two decades later, that hope barely a memory, the nation brought thousands here again, this time to build ships and train soldiers for a much larger fight. This time even the city of Vancouver reeled, for the effort brought a new sociology. Kaiser's shipyard workforce included women in record numbers and in unprecedented industrial jobs, and there were hundreds of new African American workers as well.

The hierarchies in both war eras mixed military and corporate structures, first at the great spruce mill, 1917–1918, and again in the shipyards, 1942–1945.

As a military and industrial place during the world wars, Vancouver oriented itself to shift work, the needs of recruited soldiers, and the families of shipyard workers. Especially during World War II, the community of workers and soldiers spilled over to adjacent landscapes in Vancouver, Portland, and Clark County. The need for child care, medical services, and housing created solutions that have not been duplicated since. We know something about these people's lives, but not enough, even though historians are collecting oral histories as part of the ongoing effort to document the lives of people who lived in this place. We are much more likely to know details of the generals and their families—men like Gen. Thomas Anderson and Gen. George C. Marshall—who lived in the stately houses on Officers Row.

Those houses are historic and part of the reason for preserving this place. They make it a historic landscape. But the buildings on Officers Row, the reconstructed Fort Vancouver, the preserved airstrip at Pearson Field, and the historic structures at Vancouver Barracks are only "stages" where people made history. Preserving them and this open space is pretext and context for learning about our shared past in this region of the nation. An exploration of events and people on the Vancouver National Historic Reserve is fully reason enough to preserve this landscape, and it exists as an open invitation for visitors to pursue its history.

William L. Lang, director
Center for Columbia River History,
Vancouver, Washington

GEN. O.O. HOWARD HOUSE: VANCOUVER NATIONAL HISTORIC RESERVE ⌒ Gen. Oliver Otis Howard—Civil War recipient of the Medal of Honor, proponent of higher education for African Americans, and leading founder of Howard University in Washington, D.C.—ordered a new house built (*opposite*) at Vancouver Barracks in August 1878. Howard served as commander of the Department of the Columbia from 1874 to 1880. During the last two years of his assignment in the Northwest, he lived in this house with his wife, Elizabeth, and their six youngest children.

The Vancouver *Independent* described General Howard's new home, which was equipped with a telephone, as "the finest dwelling house north of the Columbia." Howard recalled in his *Autobiography* that when he and Lizzie moved in during the second week of January 1879, they occupied it with "comfort and satisfaction."

After 1887, this home served as the residence for the post commander. In the 1930s, the army made alterations to the structure to accommodate housing for several officers. Major remodeling occurred during World War II to enlarge the building for use as an Officers Club. A fire in 1986 left it vacant. The city of Vancouver acquired the property from the army and completed renovation of the house in 1998 to use as a visitor center for the historic reserve. The main floor of the building contains the museum exhibit "One Place across Time," which depicts the reserve's nationally significant story.

Gen. O.O. Howard House, Vancouver National Historic Reserve Visitor Center

Following renovation by the city of Vancouver, the Howard House opened as a visitor center for the historic reserve. Offices are located on the second floor.

Larry Rank

National Archives

Plans and Elevation of Quarters for the General Commanding the Department of the Columbia at Fort Vancouver, Washington Territory

Typical of commanders' domiciles throughout the United States, the house included workrooms and servants' quarters at the rear. The building plans show that the army authorized $10,000 for construction.

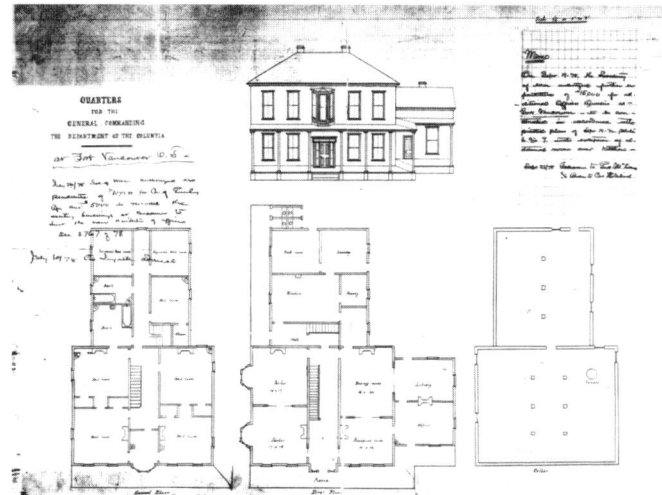

11

Gen. Oliver Otis Howard (1830–1909)

Educated at Bowdoin College and West Point, Howard spent his entire career in the U.S. Army, save for a few years following the Civil War. Pres. Abraham Lincoln appointed him head of the Freedmen's Bureau, a new agency providing education and assistance to former slaves.

Post Commander's Home, c. 1890

This graceful residence hosted many social events during its early years. Former president Ulysses S. Grant visited in October 1879. The following October, General Howard welcomed U.S. Pres. Rutherford B. Hayes.

Howard House Interior after Renovation

The "One Place across Time" exhibit opened to the public on October 31, 1998. The west parlor is shown here.

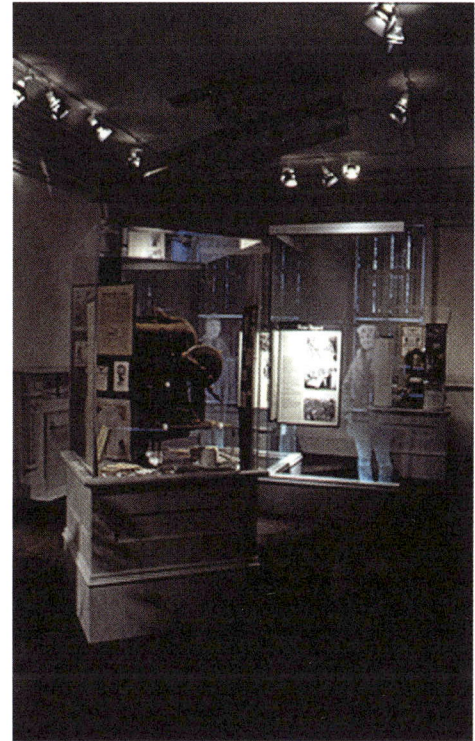

City of Vancouver

Howard House Interior prior to Renovation

This view shows the west parlor in 1996.

City of Vancouver

13

"One Place across Time," illustration by Evelyn Hicks

Vancouver National Historic Reserve

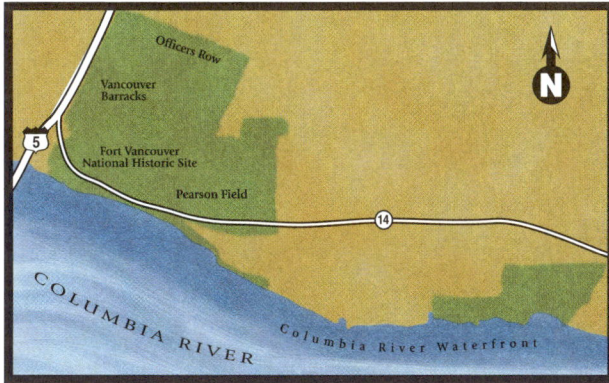

ONE PLACE ACROSS TIME ⌐ For centuries, the north shore of the Columbia River, near its confluence with the Willamette River, has been the setting of human activity of far-reaching import. This site—home to Native peoples, focus of British and American exploration, objective of traders, destination of American settlers, western outpost of U.S. military operations, birthplace of Northwest aviation, and supplier of critical resources for two world wars—offers a truly enduring legacy of *one place across time.*

In 1996, Congress established the Vancouver National Historic Reserve in recognition of the significance of this site, ensuring its preservation for future generations. Fort Vancouver National Historic Site, Vancouver Barracks and Officers Row, Pearson Field, and the Columbia River waterfront comprise the main features of the historic reserve. It is jointly managed by the National Park Service, the city of Vancouver, the U.S. Army, and the state of Washington.

The stories presented in this exhibition reflect the contributions of many women and men who lived and worked in this preserved urban landscape, which has remained remarkably unchanged during the last 150 years.

CHAPTER ONE
THE COLUMBIA RIVER

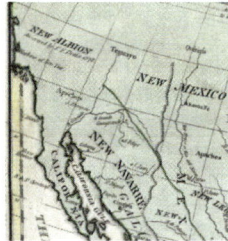

THE GREAT RIVER ⁐ One of the world's great waterways, the Columbia River has shaped human life for thousands of years. Native peoples lived and traded along the river for 10,000 years, thriving in this rich natural world.

The Columbia River flows for more than 1,200 miles and collects water from a quarter-million square-mile basin. The river is a defining geographic feature around which the history of the Pacific Northwest revolves. It has helped forge the region's economy and politics.

Oregon Historical Society, neg.#21583

Passage of The Dalles, 1867
by Carleton E. Watkins

Carleton Watkins, among the preeminent landscape photographers of the nineteenth-century American West, visited the Columbia in 1867. This stark, dramatic landscape, barren of trees and people, echoes the power of the river. The word "Dalles" comes from the French and referred to the rock formations through which the river passed. Twentieth-century dams later plugged the river and drowned this primeval view.

17

Fishing on the Columbia, 1897
by Benjamin Gifford

Benjamin Gifford operated a photography studio in the town of The Dalles, Oregon. He recorded some of the most memorable images of the Columbia and its Native inhabitants at the century's turn.

Vancouver National Historic Reserve Trust

A Chinook Traveling Lodge, with a View of Mount Hood, 1845
by Paul Kane

Canadian artist Paul Kane traveled the West from 1845 to 1848. His journey across North America from Toronto to the Pacific still stands as one of the most ambitious sketching trips in the history of painting. His remarkable body of work provides a valuable visual record from a time before photography. Kane's subjects included Indians and their homes, ceremonies, and customs, all from a period when traditional Native lifeways were still largely intact.

While away from their homes, Chinookans lived in temporary lodges made of poles covered with rushes.

Stark Museum of Art

NATIVE PEOPLES: AT HOME ALONG THE RIVER ᔥ Long before Europeans and Americans came to the Northwest coast, Native groups lived along the river and adapted to the natural surroundings. Seasons determined their fishing, hunting, and gathering activities. They gained an intimate knowledge of the landscape. Their lives centered on villages sharing kinship and common linguistic ties. A rich oral tradition reflected value systems and taught basic beliefs. Respect for the land and a practical understanding of the environment passed from one generation to the next.

Royal Engineers Library

Indian Lodges at The Dalles, 1860

This photo, taken by the British North American Boundary Commission survey crew, is the oldest known image of this area. A great Native fishery and trade center had existed here for 10,000 years. Highly developed trade and transportation networks linked the people who lived here to other regional Native groups, allowing communication between distant cultures.

MAKING THINGS ON THE RIVER ◌ Lower Columbia River tribes obtained raw materials from their environment or through trade. With stone, wood, horn, plant fibers, bone, and metal, they fashioned their household implements and wares. The long, flexible roots of spruce trees could be sewn and woven into baskets and clothing. Cattails, plentiful in shallow water, provided rushes for weaving into mats. Beads and metal, acquired in trade, became ornaments or tools. Stones were crafted into a variety of useful implements.

Below the Cascades, Columbia River, with Indian Fishing
by Paul Kane

Salmon played an integral role in the Native economy. Indians had many ways of catching fish. Here a Native is shown using a platform and a dip net.

Preserving the fish by means of drying enabled these trading cultures to exchange surplus food for other useful goods.

Fishing Columbia River

20

Clark County Museum and Oregon Historical Society (center)

Upper Cowlitz Coiled Willow and Cedar Root Basket with Bear Grass Imbrication *(right)*

Baskets were made in a variety of shapes and sizes for different purposes. Storage, carrying, and cooking were typical uses. Paul Kane noted that some were "woven so closely, as to serve all the purposes of a pail, in holding and carrying water."

This watertight container is an example of a well-made, sturdy utility basket. The design—probably geometric—has been worn away.

Wasco Root Bag *(center)*

The soft, round-shaped, twined carrying bags such as the one shown here are often called "sally bags." The earliest use of this term was by nineteenth-century artist George Catlin, who described the bags as utilitarian containers employed by Indians as they "sallye forthe" on their journeys.

This elegantly designed basket shows a high level of craftsmanship. The geometric motifs representing mountains and birds are typical of mid–Columbia River peoples.

Klickitat Basket, Coiled Cedar Root with Bear Grass Imbrication *(left)*

Women did most basket making during the winter months, after food had been gathered for the year. Baskets were often made in uniform sizes, to provide measurable units for trading purposes. Carrying straps or fern covers were looped through "ears" along the rim.

This is an excellent example of a traditional Klickitat picking basket with mountain and figure motifs.

Lithics

Clark County Museum

These groundstone tools include a rare basalt club (second from left), a pointed club of andesite (second from right), a basalt mortar and pestle (top center), a basalt axe (left), and two net weights (center and right).

Indians used pestles to break up, mash, and grind food. Women and children gathered roots, nuts, seeds, and berries. Wapato root, which is similar to the potato, could be ground into flour. Coastal and Columbia River Indians also used such tools as weights for nets as they seined for fish.

Stark Museum of Art

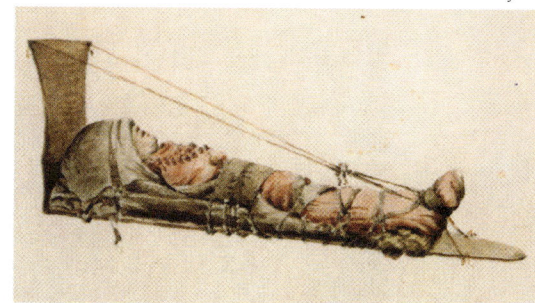

Chinook Child Undergoing Process of Head Flattening
by Paul Kane

Tribes of the lower Columbia compressed their babies' foreheads with a special cradleboard. The process did not harm the child, and the resulting permanent slope of the forehead was considered a mark of prestige, visibly distinguishing slave from nonslave.

American Antiquarian Society

Nisqually, Half Caste Indians Gambling
by Henry J. Warre

Indians in the Northwest enjoyed gambling games, especially during the long winters. In one game, a player passed a decorated bone rapidly from one hand to another. A second player tried to guess which hand held the marked bone. Players used beaver teeth to keep score. Paul Kane observed: "A Chinook will play at this simple game for days and nights together, until he has gambled away everything he possesses, even to his wife."

TRADERS OF THE COLUMBIA ⌒ Chinookans along the lower Columbia were expert traders, and women played a role in the trading process. As early Scot trader Alexander Ross noted, "The women are as actively employed as the men."

Indians lived in permanent villages united by marriage and language. They brought surplus goods to exchange at the Dalles. Many Northwest tribes practiced slavery. Some slaves were purchased, others seized in enemy raids.

Trading on the Columbia
by John Clymer

Trade would not have been possible without reliable means of transportation. Chinook tribes built many types of canoes for different purposes. Canoes measured forty to fifty feet long and could carry thirty people.

John Clymer Museum

Coiled Utility Basket

Women often decorated their woven goods with overweaves of contrasting bear grass, bracken, or maidenhair fern. This method of basket decoration, unique to limited areas of the Northwest, is called "imbrication" (derived from the Latin word for tile), since the stitch gives the basket a tilelike appearance. Columbia River tribes preferred geometric designs but used animal or human forms as well. This basket may have been used to gather acorns.

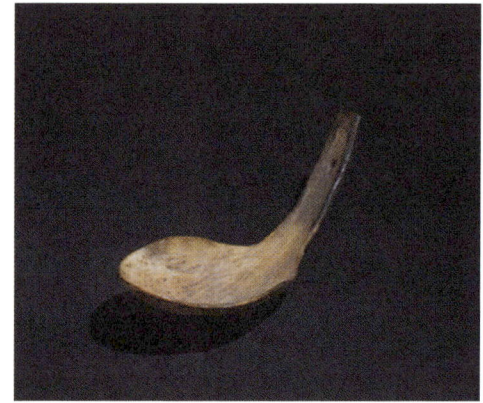

Clark County Museum

Clark County Museum

Horn Spoon

Chinooks made many of their household implements, such as this spoon, from the horns of mountain sheep.

Penny Baz Collection

Zoomorphic Basalt Carving

This carving, which may represent a sturgeon, was found around 1910 at the site of the Shoto village at Vancouver Lake. It is a remarkable example of Native stone art.

A Cascade Indian, 1847
by Paul Kane

This sketch was made about forty miles east of Fort Vancouver. Indians referred to the area around Vancouver variously as Sketcútxat or Katchutequa ("the plain"), and to the Columbia as Nch'i-Wána ("the big river").

Kane wrote of the Cascade Indians: "The men of this tribe do not tattoo, but paint their faces like other Indians."

Sally Wakygus, Lyle, Washington, 1901
by Lily E. White

This rare image, printed from the original glass-plate negative, shows a mid Columbia Indian woman posed with a partially finished coiled cedar-root basket.

Diseases brought by white traders drastically reduced aboriginal populations. A hundred years after the first recorded contact in 1775, epidemics had killed more than 80 percent of the region's Native people. By the time Lewis and Clark came downriver in 1805, one-half had perished from smallpox alone. Waves of malaria, measles, and influenza during the nineteenth century emptied many villages along the lower Columbia.

Interior of a Chinook Lodge, 1847
by Paul Kane

Five to fifteen families lived together in large rectangular houses built of split-cedar boards and posts. Raised sleeping platforms surrounded the interior, where smoke from a central fire pit escaped through a roof opening.

On the Coast of North America: Voyages of Discovery & Commerce

The remote lands of the Northwest coast of North America were among the last places on earth to be explored by Europeans. After Christopher Columbus's fifteenth-century voyage to the New World, men of courage, determination, and skill traveled for years on journeys to unknown and uncharted lands. Following many dreams, interests, and ambitions, driven by curiosity and financial gain, they came to the grand arc of the North Pacific and the fog-shrouded Northwest coast.

Using new navigation technology, European nations mounted successful maritime expeditions in the eighteenth century. These voyages of discovery revolutionized understanding of the natural world. Persistent hopes for a "Northwest Passage" or a "Great River of the West" that would extend across the continent fired the imaginations of early explorers. The nation that found these coveted water routes could expect to control the North American trade between Europe and Asia.

Beeswax

Trade ships from many nations (Spain, Russia, England, and the young United States) came to the Northwest coast during the eighteenth century. Indians who lived along the coast before recorded contact had a legend of "drifting white people," suggesting the possibility of even earlier visitors to their shores.

Most likely this wax came from a wrecked Spanish galleon on the Manila–Mexico trade route. Many wax blocks bear the date of 1679. The Spanish used the wax in the manufacture of candles, but it was of little use to Indians and was typically discarded along the beach.

"North America in Its Present Divisions," 1790

This eighteenth-century map shows parts of the Northwest coast in greater detail than earlier maps. The "River of the West" is still portrayed as a direct route across the continent.

Oregon Historical Society

Oregon Historical Society, neg.#27165

Chinese Mandarin Wearing Sea-Otter Robe

Wealthy Chinese wore elegant robes lined with the soft, rich fur of the sea otter. British Capt. James Cook, on his third scientific voyage around the world (1776–1779), obtained the pelts of many sea otters in trade with Indians on the Northwest coast. His crew discovered the high value placed on the pelts in Canton. Called "soft gold," a single pelt might sell for as much as $200. The fine pelts of this playful marine mammal shaped the course of worldwide trade in the eighteenth and nineteenth centuries.

View of Canton Harbor, c. 1800

A high wall with secure gates separated the city of Canton from traders in the port. Behind the gates were "hongs," offices and warehouses for cargo. Chinese merchants strictly controlled the trade.

Following Captain Cook's discoveries, a triangular global trade drew British and Boston ships to the Northwest coast and to China.

Peabody & Essex Museum

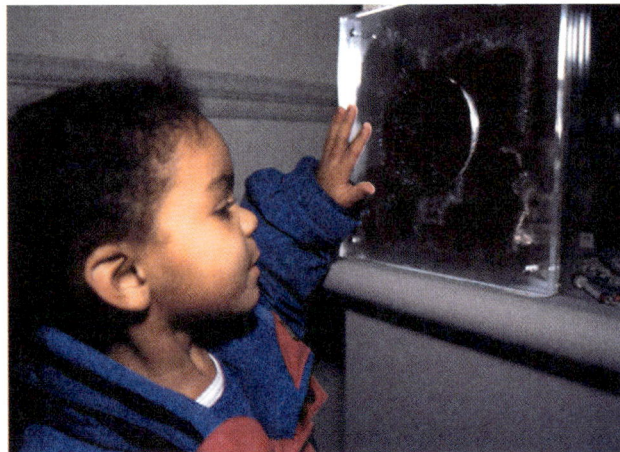

Sea-Otter Fur

A young visitor touches the sea-otter fur in a hands-on exhibit at the Howard House.

Sea-otter pelts commanded extraordinary prices in China. They were prized for their warmth and luxurious quality. Hunted almost to extinction, sea otters became a protected species in the twentieth century and are now repopulating their shallow, coastal habitats.

MARITIME FUR TRADE ∽ Business ventures in the young United States financed voyages to the Northwest coast in hopes of turning a fine profit. U.S. trading ships joined an international array of vessels from England, Spain, and Russia, all seeking fortune and empire. At the close of the eighteenth century Robert Gray, a Boston trader, crossed a treacherous bar and located the "Great River of the West."

Columbia Rediviva
by Frederick S. Cozzens

The ship *Columbia Rediviva*, or "Columbia Reborn," made two trading voyages around the world between 1787 and 1793. The *Columbia* was the first American vessel to circumnavigate the globe. Robert Gray, a Boston sea captain, made these journeys to barter for furs. On May 11, 1792, Gray and his men entered an inlet and found it to be the mouth of a great river. John Boit, eighteen-year-old fifth mate on the *Columbia*, wrote in his journal: "We directed our course up this noble river in search of a village."

Gray and his crew charted the river and traded with its people; Gray named the water course "Columbia's River," after his ship.

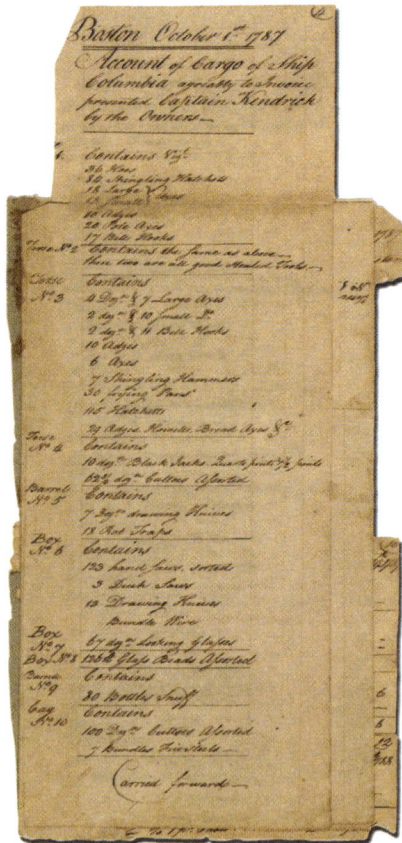

Columbia River Bicentennial Commission

Columbia Cargo List, Boston, October 1787

Columbia's holds contained an assortment of cargo used by the crew to barter for furs on the Northwest coast. In Canton, they exchanged furs for tea, silks, and other Chinese goods valued on the American market.

Longitudinal Section of the *Columbia*

by Evelyn Hicks

Little is known about the construction of this famous ship, save the dimensions and burthen (83 feet long, 212 tons burthen, or carrying capacity). The *Columbia* may have looked something like this.

Trade Beads and Brass Rings

Glass beads, buttons, coins, and brass rings brought by Euro-American traders pleased Native tastes and soon were an important part of the trade. These articles were found on the site of Fort Vancouver, the Hudson's Bay Company supply depot and trading post.

Dentalia Shell Necklace

Native groups throughout the Northwest used tusk-shaped shells, known as "haiqua," as currency. Dentalium shells formed an important part of Native trade. They were found only off the shores of Vancouver Island.

Penny Baz Collection

A Chart Showing Part of the Coast of Northwest America, 1792

George Vancouver, who had sailed with Captain Cook, led a scientific expedition between 1791 and 1795. He published his careful surveys in an atlas in 1798. The lower-right corner of this map shows Lt. William Broughton's approximation of the Columbia River, extending nearly 110 miles upstream.

ACROSS NORTH AMERICA ⸙ Robert Gray's entrance into the Columbia River in May 1792 established a claim to the Oregon Country for the United States. Gray gave his simple chart of the river to British Capt. George Vancouver, who was then exploring off the Northwest coast. In October of that same year, British Lt. William Broughton, sailing with Vancouver, crossed Columbia's bar on HMS *Chatham*. These brief visits ushered in a tide of events that would forever change the river, its shores, and its people.

Vancouver's *Voyages*, published in 1798, and Alexander MacKenzie's *Voyages from Montreal*, published in 1802, sparked wide interest. U.S. Pres. Thomas Jefferson read both accounts. These books influenced Jefferson's decision to send Meriwether Lewis and William Clark on a transcontinental expedition. Jefferson instructed the leaders of America's first scientific expedition to map their way carefully, to describe and send back specimens of nature, and to observe and befriend all Native peoples they met along the way. Their journey helped inaugurate Euro-American expansion into the American West.

Salmonberry, 1814
by Frederick Pursh

Though Lewis and Clark are best remembered as America's most celebrated team of explorers, they also made valuable contributions to science. As pioneering naturalists, Lewis and Clark recorded 178 plants and 122 animals that were new to Western science at that time. Scientists subsequently named several species after the explorers.

In 1807, Meriwether Lewis turned over his entire herbarium, collected on the expedition, to Frederick Pursh, a young German botanist. Pursh was hired to prepare drawings and arrange specimens of plants for the publication of Lewis and Clark's journals.

Academy of Natural Sciences

Sage Grouse or "Cock of the Plains"
by William Clark

This bird species was observed by Lewis and Clark near the headwaters of the Missouri River and on the plains of the Columbia.

Fort George, Astoria, 1839

This engraving was made from a drawing attributed to Edward Belcher, captain of HMS *Sulphur*, in his account of journeys to the Northwest coast.

In 1810, Boston traders Nathan, Jonathan and Abiel Winship tried unsuccessfully to settle on the Columbia River near today's Clatskanie, Oregon. The next year, the Pacific Fur Company, owned by New York businessman John Jacob Astor, established a trading post named Fort Astoria. Astoria was the first permanent settlement founded by Americans west of the Mississippi River. Fort Astoria became Fort George when the British North West Company purchased it in 1813.

CHAPTER TWO

THE HUDSON'S
BAY COMPANY

A View of London, 1842

by Thomas Shotter Boys

> Company control emanated from London, where the Governor and Committee set policy. Good management by the proprietors brought shareholders handsome profits most years.

A ROYAL CHARTER IN 1670 ⌇ Shortly after the first European settlers colonized eastern North America, Pierre Radisson and Sieur Des Groseilliers, two entrepreneurial Frenchmen who had been trapping in the interior Great Lakes and southern Hudson Bay region, proposed their ideas in England for a British fur monopoly. Thus began the venture known as the "Governor and Company of Adventurers of England Trading into Hudson's Bay."

Chartered by the British crown, the Hudson's Bay Company came to enjoy, during the next two centuries, imperial powers and monopoly privileges in the remote regions of Canada, where it dominated the western inland fur trade. The trade monopoly extended over $1^1/_2$ million square miles of territory.

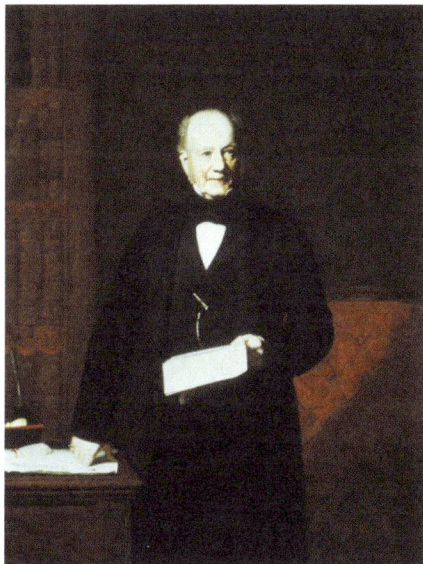

George Simpson (1786–1860), Governor of Rupert's Land

George Simpson, a Scotsman, was an administrator of exceptional talent. Imaginative vision and an ability to grasp detail and analyze economic situations produced in Simpson an "uncanny instinct for manipulating men" and shrewdly judging people, according to historian David Lavender. By 1826, Simpson had risen in the organization to be governor for all HBC operations in North America. For forty years, he ruled an empire, answerable only to the London Governor and Committee.

Known as the "little emperor," Simpson kept up a demanding pace in the field, often traveling as much as a hundred miles in a sixteen-hour day. This portrait of Sir George was painted following his investiture as a knight in 1841.

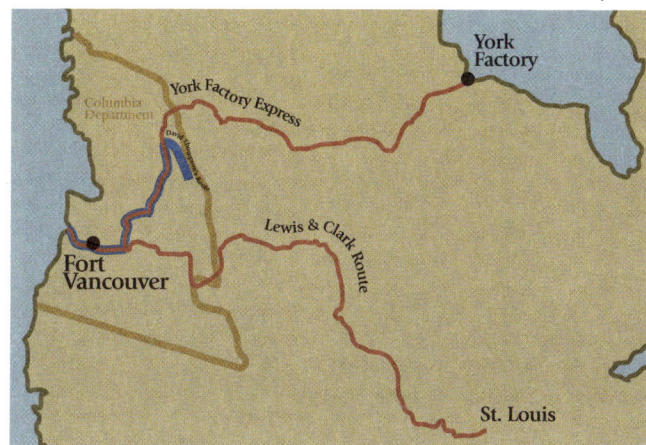

Map of Hudson's Bay Company Operations in North America

This map shows forts and express routes from York Factory on Hudson Bay to the Columbia Department in the Oregon Country. Note the route of North West Company employee David Thompson. Many scholars consider Thompson (1770–1857) among the world's finest land geographers. This "Nor'Wester" was the first person to chart the entire length of the Columbia River, arriving at the river's mouth in 1811, where he found a post—Fort Astoria—already established by John Jacob Astor's Pacific Fur Company.

Thompson pioneered the route, later known as the "York Factory Express," that served as the overland communication lifeline between Fort Vancouver and York Factory on Hudson Bay, more than 3,000 miles away.

EXPANSION ACROSS THE CONTINENT ⟲

At first, the Hudson's Bay Company was essentially a marine operation. Indians brought furs to a chain of trading posts, or "factories," along the west coast of Hudson Bay. Supply ships brought provisions and trade goods, then sailed back to England with furs. As fur resources along the bay were depleted to satisfy European and American fashion appetites, outposts penetrated into the interior, linked by navigable waterways and short portages.

Sir Alexander Mackenzie (1764–1820)
by Thomas Lawrence

Born in the Outer Hebrides Islands of Scotland, in 1779 Mackenzie came to work for the North West Company in the North American fur trade. In 1793, Mackenzie became the first white man to cross North America, a dozen years before Lewis and Clark. He reached the Pacific Ocean in present-day British Columbia and wrote this message on a rock: "Alexander Mackenzie, from Canada by land, the 22nd of July, 1793." Mackenzie missed by a few weeks meeting Capt. George Vancouver, who was then surveying the coast.

Norway House
by Paul Kane

The London directors instructed George Simpson to establish a depot at Norway House, north of Lake Winnipeg, as an intermediate station between York Factory, on Hudson Bay, and the western districts. A series of posts across the continent handled a steady exchange of furs and trade goods supplied from England.

The Establishment of Fort Vancouver

In 1824, the HBC's Columbia Department consisted of four main fur-trading posts: Fort George, at the mouth of the Columbia River; Fort Nez Percé (Walla Walla); and, farther north, Spokane House and Kootenai House. The Hudson's Bay Company had acquired these posts from the North West Company, its former rival in North America, when the two firms merged in 1821.

The Columbia Department was at first not profitable, and the Governor and Committee were prepared to give it up. But then, in 1824, they directed George Simpson to gather information on the region and recommend a course of future action. Simpson had planned to go to England to marry that year. Instead, he came west, and his trip resulted in far-reaching changes in the company's westernmost operations.

Fort Vancouver became the main supply depot and administrative headquarters of the Columbia Department, hub of all company activities west of the Rocky Mountains. Its reach extended over 400,000 square miles from Russian Alaska to Mexican California, and from the Continental Divide to the Pacific Ocean. John Dunn wrote in 1845 that "Fort Vancouver is then the grand mart and rendezvous for the Company's trade and servants . . . on the Pacific."

Dr. John McLoughlin (1784–1857)

For twenty years, Chief Factor McLoughlin, known to Natives as the "White-headed Eagle" because of his prematurely white hair, ably ruled the Columbia Department. He managed an empire that reached from Honolulu and California to Alaska and the Rockies. Trained as a physician, McLoughlin stood six feet, four inches in height and was a stern but benevolent man. Impatient and stubborn, he occasionally flew into "ungovernable rages." His integrity and "grandeur of character . . . lifted him out of the ranks of ordinary men," in the words of historian John Hussey.

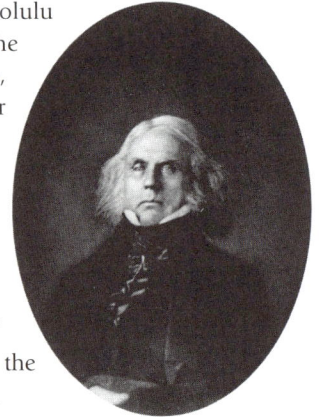

from Adventures of Oregon: A Chronicle of the Fur Trade, *1921*

Ivory-headed, Brass-tipped Cane

Dr. John McLoughlin brought this cane from Canada in 1824. The cane became the property of McLoughlin's granddaughter and was given by her to the Oregon Historical Society in 1901.

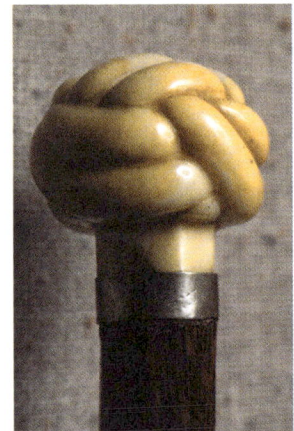

Oregon Historical Society

Fort Vancouver

by James Madison Alden

Governor Simpson ordered Fort George to be abandoned and Fort Vancouver established about a hundred miles upstream. The site had been called Belle Vue Point ("beautiful view") and Jolie Prairie ("pretty meadow") by earlier explorers and voyageurs. Lt. William R. Broughton wrote: "The adjacent country, extending from its banks, presented a most beautiful appearance."

The decision to locate in what became Vancouver was, in part, a political strategy designed to keep territory north of the Columbia River under British rule. Simpson also wanted to develop agriculture, not only to supply the needs of the posts but as a profitable branch of the export trade. Simpson placed John McLoughlin, formerly a North West Company employee, in charge.

HUDSON'S BAY COMPANY: MATERIAL CULTURE ᴄ An estimated 1¹/₂ million artifacts have been excavated at Fort Vancouver, the largest recovered collection of Hudson's Bay Company archaeological material in the world. These artifacts provide valuable information about the social and economic activities of the people living and working in the region 175 years ago.

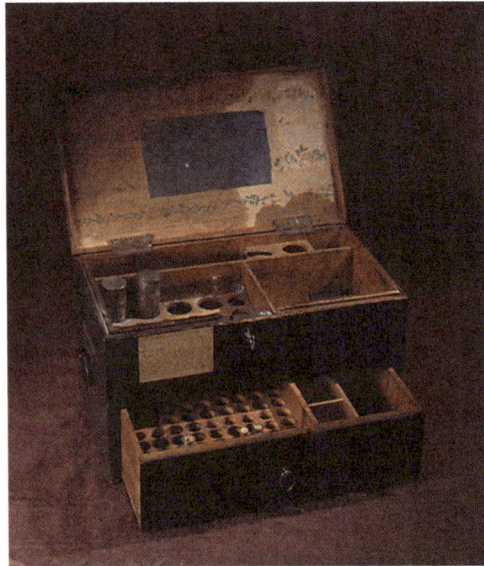

Oregon Historical Society

Medicine Chest

The Hudson's Bay Company maintained both a hospital and a dispensary for the Columbia Department at Fort Vancouver, staffed by at least one doctor. By the mid-nineteenth century, treatment of illnesses, injuries, and diseases had become technical, requiring the skills of trained doctors, surgeons, and pharmacists.

This medical chest was brought to the Oregon Country from Scotland in 1840 by Dr. Forbes Barclay, graduate of the Royal College of Surgeons in London. Barclay was physician and surgeon at Fort Vancouver from 1840 to 1850. In 1850, he moved to Oregon City and remained there until his death in 1873. The case contains ivory-mounted specimen slides for microscope viewing.

Book of Common Prayer, 1775

This Church of England prayer book belonged to John Stanger, a Hudson's Bay Company millwright. The company briefly employed a chaplain at Fort Vancouver. The Reverend Herbert Beaver and his wife, Jane, lived at Fort Vancouver from 1836 to 1838. But when Beaver clashed with John McLoughlin, he was relieved of his post and returned to England. One historian has remarked that Reverend Beaver "lacked the passionate love of soul which is the mark of a true missionary."

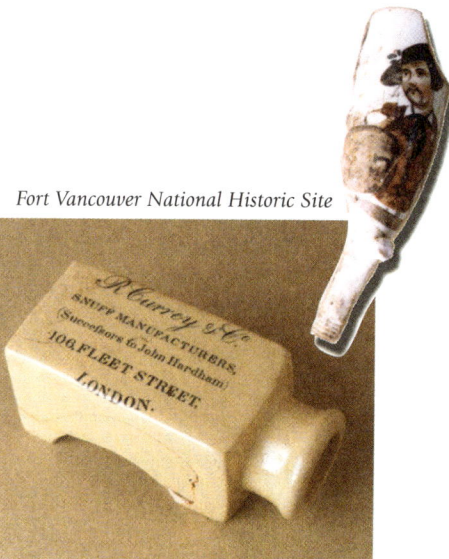

Clark County Museum

Fort Vancouver National Historic Site

Ceramic Snuff Bottle from Robert Currey & Co. and Clay Pipe Parts

Fermented, ground, and flavored tobaccos were packaged for use as snuff. The most popular method for enjoying tobacco was pipe smoking. Most fired clay pipes were made in England or Scotland, though some were imported from France and Holland.

Gosnell's "Cherry Tooth Paste," Earthenware Jar

The jar boasts: "Beautifying and Preserving the Teeth and Gums" and "Patronized by the Queen."

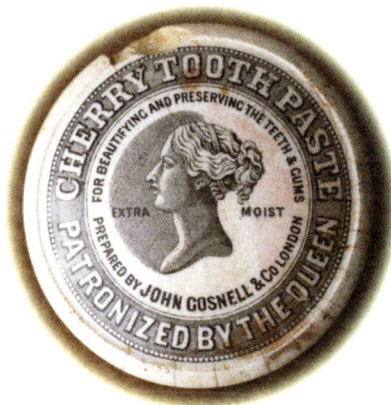

Vancouver National Historic Reserve Trust

FUR BRIGADES ~ The Hudson's Bay Company sent out trapping brigades that spent winters in the field. Working alone or in small groups, the trappers would emerge in the spring with a rich harvest of furs.

The arrival of the brigades was a grand event at Fort Vancouver each spring. Dressed in their best and singing their boatmen songs, the trappers could be heard a mile or more from the stockade. People hurried to the riverbank to greet them.

Peter Skene Ogden (1794–1854)

Ogden, a former "Nor'Wester" from Quebec, spent almost forty years on the Pacific Coast. George Simpson hired Ogden to work for the Hudson's Bay Company and, in 1825, appointed him to lead the dangerous Snake Country trapping expeditions to the interior West. Simpson wrote that "no one in this country [is] better qualified to do it justice than Mr. Ogden."

Ogden led difficult expeditions to the shores of the Great Salt Lake and the Gulf of California, explorations that greatly increased knowledge of interior regions. His activities also contributed to the region's becoming a "fur desert."

Later, Ogden became chief factor of Fort Vancouver, sharing the duties with James Douglas following John McLoughlin's retirement to Oregon City in 1846. Ogden successfully negotiated the rescue of Whitman mission survivors in 1847, thereby helping to avert a threatened Indian war.

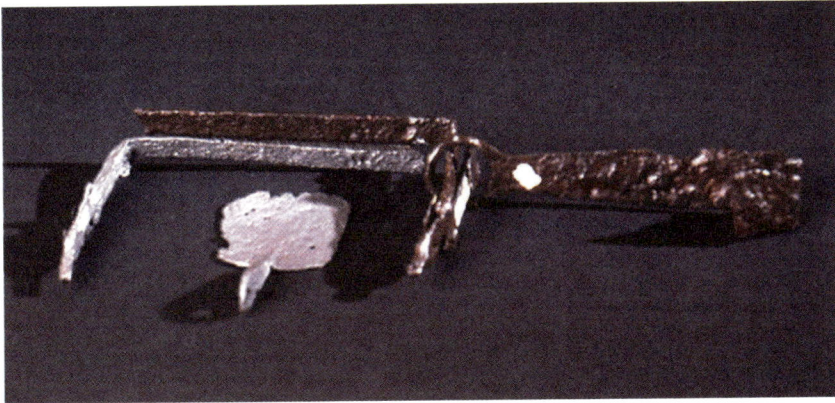

Beaver Trap Parts

Blacksmiths at Fort Vancouver forged the iron parts and steel springs of beaver traps. Traps were placed underwater, and the captured beavers were drowned.

A nineteenth-century Smithsonian Institution report noted that beaver teeth are so strong that "fingers may be snipped from the hand as though with a pair of sheers."

Fort Vancouver National Historic Site

Père DeSmet on the Athabasca River, May, 1846
by Henry J. Warre

The Society of Jesus, a Catholic order commonly referred to as the Jesuits, sent Father Pierre Jean DeSmet west in 1840 to evaluate the Oregon Country as a potential missionary region. DeSmet established the first Catholic mission in the Northwest in the Bitterroot Valley, in present-day Montana.

This painting depicts a chance meeting between Father DeSmet and Peter Skene Ogden. The meeting took place in the western Rockies, three years after Ogden and DeSmet had traveled together.

American Antiquarian Society

Fort Resolution, Northwest Territories, Trade Store Interior, c. 1908

The HBC maintained friendly relations with Indians throughout the fur-trade era. Traders at the company's posts used a barter system. HBC employee Peter Corney, wrote about the fur trade in 1821: "The chief articles of trade given in exchange to the natives on this coast are muskets, blankets, powder, shot, red paint, tobacco, beads, buttons, brass wire, with which they make bracelets and rings, and ready-made clothes. Any trifling toys please them."

Hudson's Bay Company Archives

Royal Engineers Library

Pack Mules at Fort Colvile (near Spokane, Washington)

This photo, taken by the British North American Boundary Commission survey team in 1860, reveals details of fur-trade transportation and clothing.

THE FASHIONS OF HATS ⌒ Furs were in great demand in the London market. Europe's growing commercial classes, as well as aristocrats, desired the fashionable beaver hats. Many beaver skins were needed to make the felt for these hats. A genuine "beaver," as they were called, became a fashion status symbol. By the 1820s, the hatmaking industry consumed more than 100,000 beaver pelts a year. Not everyone thought the beaver hat elegant. A writer in 1846 wondered why "the head should be covered by a black cylinder terminated at the lower edge by a spout."

Lelooska Foundation

Beaver Hat

Beaver was the most desirable fur for making felt hats. The underfur of the beaver has barblike projections that produce a strong felt. Beaver hats repel water and have a silky sheen. Some of the finest hats today are made of beaver.

from The Pictorial Gallery of Arts, Useful Arts

Hudson's Bay Company Archives

Lever-Type Fur Press at Fort Rae, c. 1908

When furs arrived at Fort Vancouver, HBC employees pressed them together in tight bales, each weighing 275 pounds, for shipment to England. Evidence indicates that a screw-type press was used at Fort Vancouver.

Hatmaking (c. 1846–1850)

This illustration shows some of the steps in the hatmaking process.

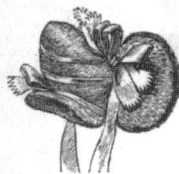

HATS, CAPS, AND BONNETS.—The largest, most fashionable, and cheapest Stocks of Hats, Caps, and Bonnets are now on sale at the Warehouses of the undersigned. List of Prices published Monthly. Country Dealers, Merchants, and Shipping supplied on the most advantageous terms.
ROBERT FRANKS AND CO., Hat and Cap Manufacturers and Patentees.

London { 140, Regent Street
62, Red Cross Street, Barbican
1, Finsbury Square.

from Penny Magazine, *London, 1835*

ROBERT FRANKS & Co. are the only Manufacturers of Hats, Caps, and Bonnets, who supply the Public at Wholesale Prices:

Gent.'s Extra Superfine Beaver Hat	21s.
„ Fine Waterproof Beaver	16s.
London Light Beaver	12s.
Gossamer Hat, 3 ounces	12s.
Drab Down Hat, 3 ounces	10s.

SILK HATS, and every description of Hats, Caps, and Bonnets, for Home Trade and Exportation, supplied at the very lowest prices.
Orders from the Country must contain a remittance, or reference for payment in London.   ROBERT FRANKS & Co.
Sole Patentees and Manufacturers of Waterproof Beaver Hats.
London: 142, Regent Street; 62, Redcross Street, City.

from Penny Magazine, *London, 1835*

Nineteenth-Century Advertisements for Beaver Hats

These ads reveal the high retail prices for hats in London and America. English novelist Jane Austen commented on the cost of hats in a letter to her sister, Cassandra, in 1801: "I . . . may suggest to Mrs. C. the notion of selling her black beaver bonnet for the relief of the poor."

HAT AND CAP ESTABLISHMENT.

S. & A. H. RHOADES.....*No. 7, Court-street,*
RESPECTFULLY inform their friends and the public, they have received a large and elegant assortment of *long* and *short napt* black HATS, of the latest London, Paris and New-York fashions, which for beauty of shape, lightness, durability and price are equal to any offered in the city—youths' Hats, of all descriptions—misses' *Beaver Bonnets*.
CAPS.
An extensive assortment of Otter, Fur Seal, Nutra and Hair Seal Caps—Patent Leather, Cloth and Silk, fancy Sporting, Military and Travelling do—Caps made to any order and of the best workmanship.
GLOVES.
London and Paris Buckskin, Doe, Beaver, Goat Skin and Kid Gloves—Fur Seal, Russia Mole and sable do.
Ladies' elegant Paris PLUMES, of all descriptions—Russia ERMINE ROBES, for ladies' dresses, some very costly. Also, sable, Russia grey, black, mock sable and white Ermine Pelerines—London Paris and Philadelphia UMBRELLAS—Hatters' Trimmings, Furs,&c.
Just received, 20 cases of HATS, of a superior quality, for $3 50,   3awistf   nov 20

from Boston Patriot and Mercantile Advertiser,
January 7, 1830

ELEGANT HATS,
AT $4 LATEST PATTERN—
CAN be bought at PECK'S HAT ESTABLISHMENT, (corner of Cornhill and Washington street) equal to those that are selling at $4 25—and for the simple reason that he has a large Factory of his own, and can afford to manufacture them at that price
ALSO—at $4—Just received from New York, SIMMS' SATIN BEAVERS, warranted his best quality and of the *latest fashion.*
LIKEWISE, by the Case, as usual, is offered the largest assortment of HATS in the city, and will be sold as low as can be bought at any other place.
april 4   W & S½—T & Thostf

from Boston Commercial Gazette, *April 5, 1832*

FORT VANCOUVER: A PERMANENT HEADQUARTERS

~ When George Simpson ordered the establishment of Fort Vancouver, he thought the location would be only temporary. He planned to locate a permanent depot in Canada, at the mouth of the Fraser River. On March 19, 1825, Simpson dedicated the fort on a defensible bluff just northeast of the later fort site, noting in his journal: "At sunrise. . . I baptised it by breaking a bottle of Rum on the Flag Staff."

Simpson had hoped that the Fraser River, closer to the source of furs, would be a reliably navigable river, but further exploration proved this hope unfounded. He was forced to conclude that the Columbia was "the only navigable River to the Interior from the Coast" and was thus essential for the company's business west of the mountains. In 1829, Fort Vancouver became the permanent army departmental depot, and the fort was relocated still closer to the river.

David Douglas (1799–1834)

Many scientists, artists, explorers, missionaries, and settlers were welcomed at Fort Vancouver. Scottish botanist David Douglas visited the fort in 1825 and 1830. The Royal Horticultural Society sent Douglas on two collecting journeys to the Northwest, where he discovered many new animal and plant species. The Douglas fir is named for him. Natives called Douglas the "Grass Man" for his tireless collecting and cataloging of plants. Douglas was the first of a long line of distinguished travelers

Oregon Historical Society, neg. #19683

to visit and enjoy the hospitality of Fort Vancouver.

North American Boundary Commission Survey Camp at Fort Vancouver, 1860

This photo shows the interior of the fort stockade, looking west toward one of four warehouses. In 1844, approximately 60,000 pelts were stored here. At that time, all furs in the Columbia Department were brought to Fort Vancouver. In the fur warehouse, pelts were sorted, counted, beaten, and baled before shipment to England.

Fort Vancouver, Interior of the Post, Looking East, 1860

This view shows, from left: priest's house, chief factor's house, and quarters for subordinate officers and their families. The belfry sounded the hours designated for labor and rest. Neither weatherboarding nor paint softened the rustic lines of the chief factor's residence until 1841. By 1845, the year fur-trade activities peaked at the fort, there were approximately twenty-seven major structures inside the stockade—containing industries that were "required to keep in motion the vast mercantile machine," according to Capt. Henry J. Warre.

Slate Tablet Fragments

The HBC established the first school in the Oregon Country late in 1832 at Fort Vancouver. Schoolchildren and clerks used slate tablets and slate pencils for calculations.

Fire Steel and Flint, Candle Snuffer

Before the advent of safety matches, flint was struck with a fire steel to create a spark for starting fires. Candles provided light. Tallow candles, made locally, were used by the working class. Beeswax candles were imported from England.

Stoneware Ink Bottle

Originally stoppered with a cork, this bottle was used for bulk ink storage. The ink was dispensed from this bottle into smaller inkwells and used for keeping company records.

For the many clerks of the Columbia Department, specialized items needed to be ordered from London stationery stores to fulfill the company's elaborate accounting requirements. The HBC maintained detailed written records of its operations, most of which are preserved today in the Hudson's Bay Company Archives in Winnipeg, Canada. Clerks were kept busy copying and compiling material in triplicate. To ensure against loss, two copies were sent overland to York Factory and a third on to London via the annual supply ship.

Stoneware Blacking Bottle

Traders used liquid blacking to enhance the appearance of leather, primarily shoes, boots, and harnesses.

THE PLAINS OF JOLIE PRAIRIE ∽ Under John McLoughlin's leadership, agriculture and industries grew quickly at Fort Vancouver. The chief factor wanted his department to show a profit, and he left few opportunities untried. McLoughlin kept his employees engaged at productive work. The company maintained ships, boats, large farms, and regular travel and communication with England. It carried on a great fur trade and a large export/import business, unparalleled in North America at the time. The value of imported goods for Outfit (business year) 1845, for example, was $59,923.81—today, equivalent to millions of dollars. In addition to supplying the needs of more than thirty-five posts in the department, Fort Vancouver also shipped wheat, lumber, salt salmon, sea biscuit, and dairy products to Hawaii and Russian Alaska.

By 1845, more than a thousand acres were under cultivation at Fort Vancouver, and large herds of livestock grazed on the nearby plains. The company also established manufacturing industries, such as boatbuilding, blacksmithing, and sawmilling.

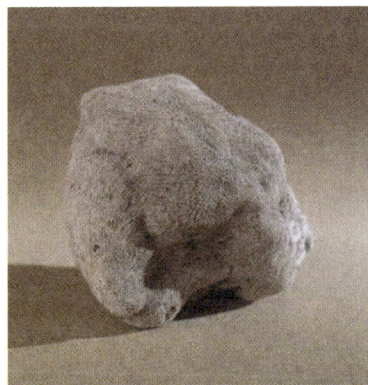

Fort Vancouver National Historic Site

Hawaiian Coral

The company brought coral from the Sandwich Islands as ship ballast. The coral was later burned into lime for making plastered floors and mortar for bricklaying.

Oregon Historical Society

Honolulu Harbor, 1822

by M. Louis Choris

The Sandwich Islands (Hawaiian Islands) were an important port of call for vessels trading in the Pacific. The Hudson's Bay Company established a store there to facilitate the trade.

SANDWICH ISLANDS NEWS.

VOL. I]   HONOLULU, OAHU, WEDNESDAY, JANUARY 20, 1847.   [NO. 21

OREGON PRODUCE.

FOR SALE BY C. BREWER & CO., the cargo of Am. ship MARIPOSA, from Columbia River, consisting of

231 Bbls. Superfine Flour,
138 " Willamette Salmon,
114 " Chincook do.
186 m. Shingles,
100 " feet Fir & hemlock boards, ass'd.
13 " " Spruce boards,
5 " " Weather boarding,
20 " " Fir & hemlock Scantling.
The above lumber is of superior quality.
o. 21, tf.

Oregon Historical Society, neg.#95001

Oregon Produce Advertisement,
Sandwich Island News,
January 20, 1847

This newspaper ad lists products the company shipped to Hawaii. Lomilomi salmon, a staple in any Hawaiian feast today, originated from Columbia River salmon shipped by the Hudson's Bay Company.

THE COASTAL TRADE: MARITIME ACTIVITIES OF THE HUDSON'S BAY COMPANY

Artifacts give evidence of the HBC's boatbuilding activities at Fort Vancouver. The shipyard was located adjacent to a large pond next to the wharf on the Columbia. The fort's strategic location linked the site by water to the interior and to the coast. The company had, in effect, its own private navy. Its coastal trading operations, from San Francisco to Hawaii to Canada, were important to the company's economic success.

Fort Vancouver National Historic Site

Caulking Iron, Rivets, Boat Nails, and Copper Sheathing

Beginning in the eighteenth century, copper was used to sheath or cover ships below the waterline. Copper helped waterproof the vessels and inhibit the growth of algae. Blacksmiths fabricated boat nails and other ship fittings at the fort. Evidence indicates that the rivets shown here are from the *Beaver*'s boiler. Caulking irons were used to caulk ships with oakum (stringy hemp fiber from old ropes) to keep them watertight.

Greenheart Wood from the Steamship *Beaver*

In 1836 the *Beaver*, the first steamship on the Northwest coast, arrived at Fort Vancouver from London. The *Beaver* plied the waters of the Pacific coastal trade for more than fifty years, calling at company posts on Puget Sound and many locations in British Columbia.

Vancouver National Historic Reserve Trust

Hudson's Bay Company Mill, Pacific Railroad Report

Located six miles east of the fort, near a suitable water source, the company's sawmill and gristmill kept employees busy. By 1829, the first load of lumber was shipped to Hawaii from Fort Vancouver.

Gristmill Stone Segment

The company used a circular gristmill stone to grind grain at the region's first water-powered gristmill.

Fort Vancouver Tools and Agricultural Implements

This group of items includes a saw blade from the first sawmill in the Oregon Country; a plow, used to plow fields on company farms; chisels; and blacksmith tongs, used to hold hot iron during the forging process.

Charles Wilkes (1798–1877)
by Thomas Sully

U.S. Navy Lt. Charles Wilkes led a government-sponsored maritime expedition around the world between 1838 and 1842. Wilkes lost one of his ships, the *Peacock*, when it tried to cross the Columbia River bar. Ships sometimes waited for a month or more for a good opportunity to cross this dangerous bar, and many others sank attempting to enter the river. Wilkes and his men stayed at Fort Vancouver from May to September 1841, mapping and surveying extensively in the Oregon Country. This work was important to U.S. territorial interests in the region. The botanical and ethnographic specimens the expedition brought back formed the basis of the Smithsonian Institution collections.

U.S. Naval Academy Museum

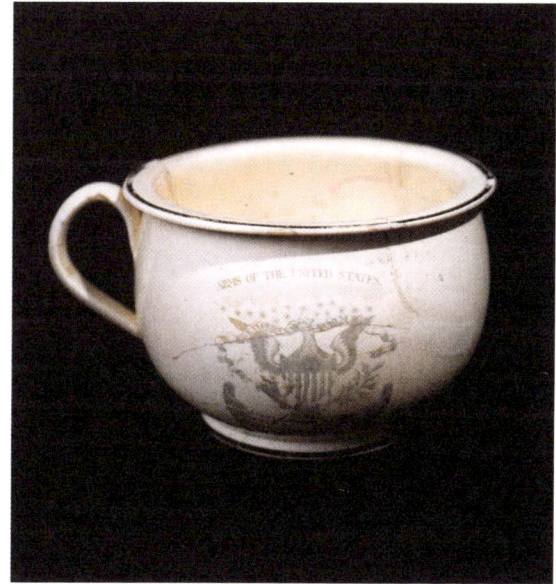

Earthenware Chamber Pot

Archaeologists excavated this pot at Fort Vancouver. It may have been manufactured specifically for the 1838–42 U.S. Exploring Expedition.

Tethering Anchor

This anchor is associated with the Hudson's Bay Company or the early U.S. Army period.

Oregon Historical Society

A DIVERSE COMMUNITY ⌖ By the 1840s, Fort Vancouver was the most important Euro-American settlement and the largest population center on the west coast of North America. About 350 employees and their families (some 900 people altogether) lived within the fort and in the village outside the palisade. It was an ethnically diverse group—French Canadians, Iroquois, Scots, English, Americans, Orkney Islanders, local Indians, and Kanakas (Hawaiians). They spoke Chinook jargon, a trade language that facilitated communication among the many groups.

Fort Vancouver National Historic Site

The Village
artist unknown

Strict rules governed each person's place in the Hudson's Bay Company social hierarchy. Clerks and officers, who came from the British Isles, formed the "gentlemen class" and lived inside the stockade. Most laborers lived in the village, just west of the fort. John Townsend, a Fort Vancouver visitor, noted in his journal: "Huts are placed in rows with broad lanes or streets between them, and the whole looks like a very neat and beautiful village."

Old Coxe, a Sandwich Islander of the Hudson's Bay Company
by Paul Kane

John Coxe was among the 122 Kanaka workers listed on Fort Vancouver's employment rosters. Coxe was said to have witnessed, as a young boy, the murder of Capt. James Cook in Hawaii in 1779. Hawaiians worked as contract laborers for the company, primarily as trappers, farmers, or sawmill hands.

Royal Ontario Museum

Chief Casanov at Fort Vancouver, 1841
by Paul Kane

Casanov was a noted warrior chief who led the Indians in the region of Fort Vancouver. As an old man, he resided principally in a lodge outside Fort Vancouver with his wives, offspring, and slaves. John McLoughlin provided Casanov with a separate table where he could dine with the gentlemen in the chief factor's mess hall.

Stark Museum of Art

Ranald McDonald (1824–1894)

McDonald was the son of Princess Sunday (daughter of Chinook Chief Concomly) and Hudson's Bay Company clerk Archibald McDonald. As a child, Ranald knew the story of three shipwrecked Japanese fishermen who had drifted across the Pacific Ocean to the Washington coast in 1834. Chief Factor McLoughlin brought the three survivors to Fort Vancouver, and a few months later sent them on to London and Macao.

McDonald later determined to visit Japan, which at that time was forbidden to all foreigners. For ten months in 1848 he lived under restriction in Japan, where he was allowed to teach English to scholars who interpreted for Commodore Matthew Perry and his crew in 1854.

Oregon Historical Society, neg.#4729

Daughters of the Country: Women in Fur-Trade Society

Women played an important role in fur-trade society. Many white traders took "country wives," a practice also referred to as marriage *à la façon du pays* ("in the manner of the country"). These marriages, encouraged by the HBC, helped to cement trading ties. Fort Vancouver's commissioned officers—John McLoughlin, James Douglas, Peter Skene Ogden—all carried on long-term "country marriages" with Indian wives. James Douglas declared that without "the many tender ties" of family, the monotonous life of a fur trader would have been unbearable.

Some traders did not hold Native women in high esteem. George Simpson had a number of liaisons with mixed-blood women whom he later abandoned.

Grand Ball at Fort Victoria, 1845
by Henry J. Warre

Dancing was a favorite pastime of the fur traders. Even though the music might be provided by a mere fiddle, the men seized upon any excuse for a break in the daily work routine.

Public Archives of Canada

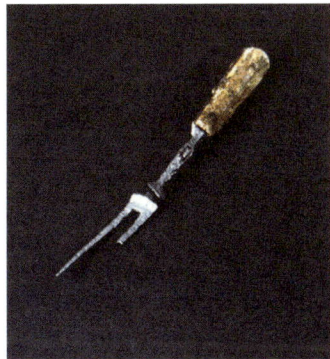

Dinnerware, Hand-decorated Chinese Export Dessert Plates, British Transfer Printed Spodeware, and Carving Fork with Forebuck Handle

In addition to the great volume of British ceramics imported to the Columbia Department, "Boston," or American, merchants returning from China brought a number of Chinese porcelains to the Sandwich Islands. Chinese potters made blue-and-white glazed ceramic ware known as "Cantonware." China for export made excellent ballast in the holds of top-heavy sailing ships on their homeward journey.

The blue-and-white designs of Ming Dynasty porcelain were quite popular in England and Holland. As early as 1625, Delft pottery factories copied the designs. Later, they inspired English Willowware.

The HBC brought European traditions to the fort, which was considered a "haven of English-style living," according to Paul Kane. The chief factor presided over formal dinners, and a wine cellar was stocked with favored clarets from Bordeaux.

Rum Bottle

The company issued rum, contained in dark olive-green "black glass" (as shown here), as a ration to its employees. Rum and tobacco were packed with furs to repel insects during shipment to London.

Ginger Jar

Chinese semiporcelain jar used for storing and transporting ginger.

Fort Vancouver National Historic Site

Harmonica Parts and Mouth Harp

Mouth harps and harmonicas were common, easily played, musical instruments.

Fort Vancouver National Historic Site

North West Company Tokens

The North West Company established several posts in the region and carried on trade during the second decade of the nineteenth century. Its representatives exchanged brass or copper tokens with Native people for furs.

Fort Vancouver National Historic Site

Hudson's Bay Company Brass Tokens

These trade tokens were used by the company at some of its posts.

Fort Vancouver National Historic Site

Buttons and Beads

Buttons were the most common clothing fasteners available. Buttons recovered from Fort Vancouver excavations include those made of metal, iron, bone, shell, ceramic, glass, rubber, and stone.

Decorative ornaments were imported primarily as items for Native trade. Vast quantities of glass beads of many varieties, colors, and sizes were shipped to the Columbia Department. Chinese beads came directly from Canton through various brokers.

Baptiste la Pierre, a French "Half-Breed" and Salmon Chief of the Colville Tribe
by British North American Boundary Commission

The men pictured here are dressed in European-style clothing and are wearing moccasins.

Women performed valuable work in fur-trade society, such as making clothes, moccasins, and snowshoes, and procuring, preparing, and preserving food. Their contributions in dressing furs and interpreting languages were also particularly important.

Christine McDonald, Daughter of Chief Trader at Fort Colvile
by British North American Boundary Commission

Native wives of fur-trade officers at Fort Vancouver dressed in the English style, but were not invited to eat with the men. Though respected and often treated fairly, women's basic role was to serve men.

Paul Kane reported that Chief Concomly, the great Chinook leader, carpeted his daughter's path ("from the canoe to the Fort [George] with sea otter skins") as a dowry when she married a British trader.

PRIESTS AND MISSIONARIES ⌐ Beginning in the 1830s, both Protestant and Catholic missionaries came to play an important part in the history of the Oregon Country.

In 1831, four Flathead Indians arrived in St. Louis seeking the white man's Book of Heaven (the Bible). This event was reported widely in the Protestant press, and subsequently the first Methodist missionaries arrived at Fort Vancouver in 1834. They received a cordial welcome from Dr. John McLoughlin and soon established missions in the region.

**Panorama of Vancouver,
St. James Mission**
by British North American Boundary Commission

This photo, taken in 1860, shows the fort's Catholic church on the right, located just northwest of the Hudson's Bay Company stockade.

The church and surrounding lands became entangled in a complicated legal controversy between the U.S. Army and the Roman Catholic Church. The case dragged on for years and was not settled until 1905. The War Department prevailed, and the church was nominally compensated for its real estate.

Royal Engineers Library

Mission Station of Rev. Elkanah Walker and Rev. Cushing Eells, Tshimakain
by Paul Kane

This mission station on the Spokane River, about seventy miles from Fort Colvile, was established in 1838. Paul Kane visited the comfortable log homes of the missionaries and their families in 1847. The mission was abandoned in 1848 because of increasing hostilities with Indians. Reverend Eells translated Christian scripture and hymns into Chinook jargon.

Dictionary of Chinook Jargon

Missionaries translated and printed Chinook trade jargon and other Native languages. Chinook jargon included words from various languages spoken by traders. For example, "Bostons" was used for sailors from the United States, and "le-pan" (from the French word *pain*) was used for "bread."

Missionaries brought the first printing press to the Oregon Country. It arrived in 1839 from the Sandwich Islands and was taken to the Lapwai mission of Henry Spalding near Fort Nez Percé (Walla Walla).

Fort Vancouver National Historic Site

Father Francis Norbert Blanchet (1795–1883) and A.M.A. Blanchet (1797–1884)

The archbishop of Quebec sent priests to serve French Canadians living in the Willamette Valley, Hudson's Bay Company employees, and Indians. These two brothers were founding leaders of the Catholic church in the Pacific Northwest. Francis arrived first, in 1838, and was later appointed archbishop of Oregon. His younger brother, A.M.A. Blanchet, served as bishop of Nisqually at Vancouver.

A Region in Dispute: England and the United States Occupy the Oregon Country, 1812–1846

At the conclusion of the War of 1812, England and the United States agreed to temporary joint occupancy of the Oregon Country. Several attempts were made throughout the 1820s to resolve the "Oregon Question" by negotiation, but each effort merely extended the period of joint occupancy.

No negotiations took place between 1827 and 1843 while Great Britain's Hudson's Bay Company strengthened its position in the region. Increasing American settlement in the Oregon Country in the 1840s and political conditions in England, however, caused international discussions to be reopened. Through compromise, the boundary was finally fixed in June 1846, in its current position at the forty-ninth parallel.

Pres. James K. Polk (1795–1849)
by Nathaniel Currier

Polk's campaign slogan of "54-40 or Fight!" proclaimed that the United States should possess the entire Oregon Country, north to latitude 54°40′, even if it meant war with Britain. In his inaugural address, Polk stated that he considered the right of the United States to the Oregon Country "clear and unquestionable."

The boundary dispute was finally settled on June 15, 1846, but the news traveled by ship via Hawaii and did not reach the Oregon Country until November 4, 1846 (when it was reported in Oregon City's newspaper, the *Oregon Spectator*).

This lithographic print of President Polk was made between 1845 and 1849. It predates the era, beginning in 1857, when the printing firm became known as Currier and Ives.

Disputed Territory of Columbia or Oregon Showing Its Limits As Settled by Different Treaties and the Boundaries Proposed by England and America

Governments of both Britain and the United States took an increasing interest in the disputed Oregon Country during the 1840s. The British government sent two officers, Lt. Henry J. Warre and Lt. Mervin Vavasour of the Royal Engineers, to Oregon in 1845–46, pretending to be private travelers on a lengthy excursion to the West. In fact, the engineers were spies carrying out a secret mission, gathering intelligence and drafting reports concerning the strategic value of the Oregon Country.

Warre and Vavasour were to take possession of Cape Disappointment and erect a fortress there to secure the Columbia River in case of war with America. Peter Skene Ogden, who had brought the officers out West, knew the true purpose of their journey and was none too taken with the pair: "I had certainly two most disagreeable companions. . . . [M. Vavasour was at times] most disquieting, particularly when under the influence of brandy and opium."

Clark County Museum

**Fort Vancouver with HMS *Modeste*
Anchored in the Columbia River, 1847**
by Paul Kane

For seventeen months (from November
30, 1845, to May 4, 1847), the eighteen-
gun sloop-of-war *Modeste*, under the
command of Thomas Baillie, and her
crew of ninety remained anchored in the
mile-wide Columbia off Fort Vancouver.
According to a contemporary account,
the ship was there as a show of force
during a difficult time—"to prevent the
American settlers [from] taking the law
into their own hands and [to] give
protection to the property of the
Hudson's Bay Company."

**Theatre Notice, Vancouver Thespiancorps,
September 6, 1853**

The crew of HMS *Modeste* brightened life at
Fort Vancouver when the officers and men
gave a series of entertainments, to which they
invited American settlers and Hudson's Bay
Company employees. These were the first
plays performed on the Pacific Coast.
Canadian artist, Paul Kane, attended these
theatricals and saved a handwritten broadside
announcing the January 5, 1847, performance.
Lts. Warre and Vavasour also saw the plays a
year earlier.

The theatrical tradition continued when
the army arrived a few years later, as shown in
this playbill.

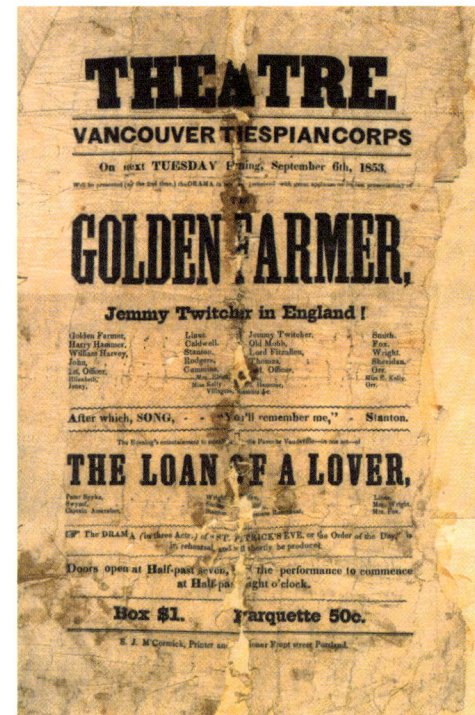

Copper Rum Measure

Quartermaster records for the *Modeste* reveal that the crew, while moored off Fort Vancouver, principally occupied themselves with repair and maintenance of the ship and sustenance of the ship's company. Some cut wood, prepared oakum, repaired sails, and made and mended clothes. Blacksmiths, rope makers, caulkers, and carpenters were kept busy. The ninety-man crew typically ate 120 pounds of fresh beef and 67 pounds of fresh vegetables daily. Food, hardware, and clothing were purchased from the stores and warehouses of the Hudson's Bay Company. A thirty-five-gallon cask of rum was opened once a week to meet the British navy's daily ration of one-half pint of rum per man, per day. The liquor was mixed with water to make "grog."

Drunkenness was punished by flogging in the Royal Navy. The *Modeste* daily remarks book for March 30, 1846, noted: "Punished Issac Burling with 36 lashes for drunkenness."

Calapooia, Arriving at Fort Vancouver with American Immigrants, 1845
by Evelyn Hicks

From 1840 to 1860, thousands of immigrants made the arduous 2,000-mile trek across the continent to inhabit the Oregon Country. The journey usually started in Missouri in the spring and took six months. Most immigrants came with families, lured by the promise of a new life in a distant land. Promotions of Oregon as the "promised land" by Boston schoolteacher Hall J. Kelley, published reports of the American Board of Commissioners for Foreign Missions, and the ideology of "Manifest Destiny" all contributed to the waves of overland immigrants that began rolling toward Oregon in the 1840s.

The final hundred miles of the journey, from The Dalles to Fort Vancouver, was often made by boat. The immigrants generally arrived in the cold, wet fall, in miserable condition. John McLoughlin received the newcomers with kindness and frequently loaned them supplies. Without his assistance, few could have lasted in the new country.

THE HUDSON'S BAY COMPANY   69

Stark Museum of Art

The Mills of Oregon City

by Paul Kane

John McLoughlin violated HBC policy by helping American settlers. He retired from the company in January 1846, moved to property he owned in Oregon City, and later became an American citizen. McLoughlin owned many of the buildings in this early view of Oregon City.

Blue and White Woven Coverlet, 1843

Reversible handwoven coverlets were typical bed coverings made in America in the nineteenth century. This coverlet was probably brought to Vancouver by early settlers arriving via the Oregon Trail.

Clark County Museum

VANCOUVER, WASHINGTON TERRITORY ⟋ Early settlers were town builders as well as farmers. However, it was not until the 1880s, when the transcontinental railroad ushered in a spectacular period of economic growth, that extensive townscapes developed. Many newcomers, initially drawn to the Hudson's Bay Company post, remained to build homes. The town of Vancouver inherited its name from Fort Vancouver and developed just west of the Hudson's Bay Company post and the U.S. military reservation. The town name, originally Columbia City, was changed in 1855 by the territorial legislature to Vancouver. Two years later Vancouver was incorporated as a city.

**Panoramic View of Vancouver,
Showing U.S. Quartermaster Depot, 1860**
by British North American Boundary Commission

This view, looking west from the Hudson's Bay Company post toward the town of Vancouver, shows little remaining of the old Fort Vancouver village area. The U.S. Army arrived in 1849 and began renting buildings from the British company and using the land. The Quartermaster Depot, on the right in this early photo, was home to Ulysses S. Grant while he was stationed in Vancouver from September 1852 to December 1853.

After 1846, the Hudson's Bay Company had wound down their Fort Vancouver operations, which were now located in U.S. territory. Department headquarters were transferred to Fort Victoria, on Vancouver Island, in 1849. Finally, on June 14, 1860, the "Honourable Company" abandoned the great fur emporium on the Columbia. The company was guaranteed "possessory rights" under the Oregon Treaty and was awarded $650,000.

Today, the Hudson's Bay Company still exists—more than three centuries after its founding—as a prosperous Canadian retail department store known as The Bay.

PERIOD OF TRANSITION, 1846–1860 ❧ The years between 1846 and 1860 represented a time of great change in Vancouver. The U.S. Army arrived, as did increasing numbers of American settlers. The Hudson's Bay Company attempted to continue its business, although that became more difficult as relations with the U.S. military deteriorated and settlers took over the company's land. The company retreated north to Victoria, in British Columbia, in 1860. In 1866 a mysterious fire burned the Hudson's Bay Company stockade and remaining buildings at Fort Vancouver.

English Iron Keys

These are believed to be the original keys to Fort Vancouver that Chief Trader James Allan Grahame turned over to U.S. Army Quartermaster Capt. Rufus Ingalls on June 14, 1860. Grahame announced he was leaving for Canada within the hour on the HBC ship *Otter*.

Vancouver, 1858

by Charles Kuchel and Emil Dresel

Many itinerant artists captured the spirit of frontier towns with bird's-eye views that were widely circulated as lithographs. Still visible in the background of this view is the Hudson's Bay Company bastion. Vignettes surrounding the principal scene provide details of the community's major buildings. Early-day residents could trade either with town merchants or at the HBC store. No structures shown here still exist. The viewmakers, Charles Kuchel and Emil Dresel, came west during the California Gold Rush.

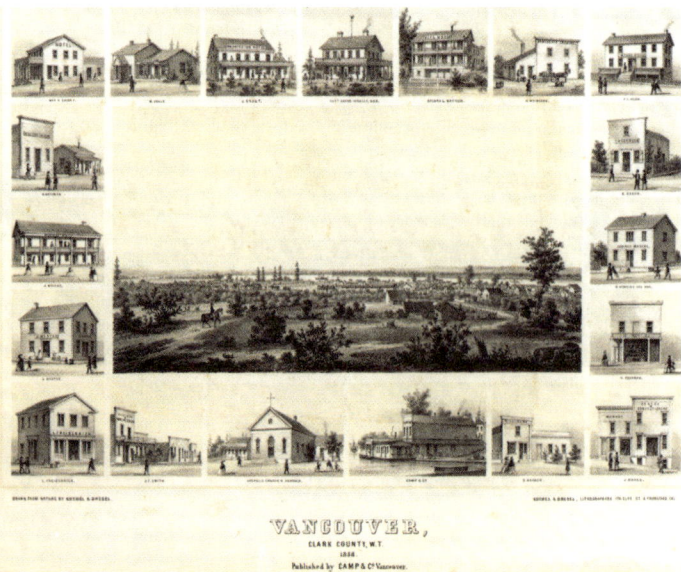

VANCOUVER,
CLARK COUNTY, W.T.
1858
Published by CAMP & Cº Vancouver.

Fort Vancouver National Historic Site

Royal Engineers Library

Zenith Telescope and Observatory Tent, Captain Darrah and Assistant

by British North American Boundary Commission

After the discovery of gold in 1856 in British Columbia, the need to survey and map the boundary accurately became obvious. Both the United States and England agreed to appoint commissioners to locate the boundary established by the Oregon Treaty of 1846. The Royal Engineers surveyed the western portion of the boundary between the United States and Canada in 1858–62.

In addition, the engineers photographed the people and country they traveled through. A collection of eighty-one photos in the Royal Engineers Library provides the earliest known photographic record of the Pacific Northwest. The American survey team loaned the Zenith telescope, visible in the photo, to the English astronomers.

C H A P T E R T H R E E
VANCOUVER BARRACKS

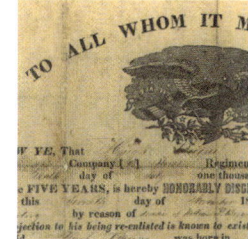

U.S. Troops Establish Camp Vancouver

In May 1849, the U.S. Army arrived at Fort Vancouver to establish its authority and military presence in the new U.S. territory. During the fall of that year, troops built a headquarters building on the bluff overlooking the Hudson's Bay Company post. This building still exists and is known today as the Grant House. During the next ten years, the army shared buildings and land with the company.

The army named its new garrison "Columbia Barracks" to distinguish it from the Hudson's Bay Company depot. Four years later, the military reservation became known as "Fort Vancouver." Many military leaders who won fame in the Civil War—Ulysses S. Grant, Phil Sheridan, George McClellan—saw service as junior officers in Vancouver in the 1850s.

from The March of the Mounted Riflemen, *1851*

March of the Regiment of Mounted Riflemen, "View from Campground," August 22, 1849

A splendid account of the U.S. Army's journey from Fort Leavenworth to Oregon City/Fort Vancouver was published as part of the *Annual Report of the Quartermaster General for Fiscal Year Ending on 30th June, 1850*. The overland troops arrived from the East on October 4, 1849. The USS *Massachusetts* had preceded the ground troops, arriving at Astoria in May under the command of Maj. John S. Hatheway.

Brass Military Spyglass

This telescope belonged to the Switzler family of early Vancouver. The Switzlers operated the first ferry on the Columbia River at Vancouver and supplied the army with goods.

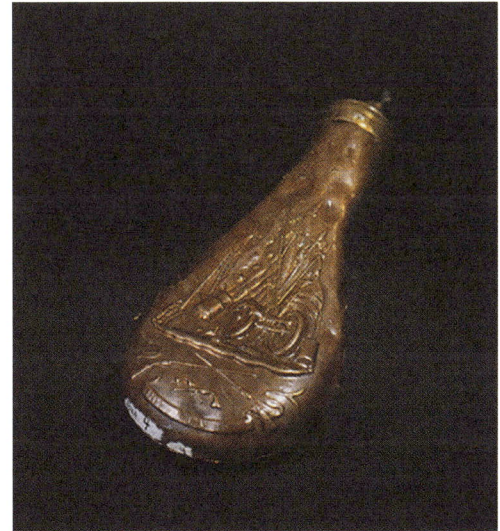

Brass Powder Flask, Colts Patent, c. 1850

This flask held powder for a flintlock gun.

Army Discharge Papers Signed by Maj. John S. Hatheway

Major Hatheway commanded the first U.S. troops in Vancouver. He sailed from the East coast on board the sailing and steaming transport *Massachusetts*. Traveling by way of the Straits of Magellan and Hawaii, this contingent reached Fort Vancouver on Sunday, May 13, 1849.

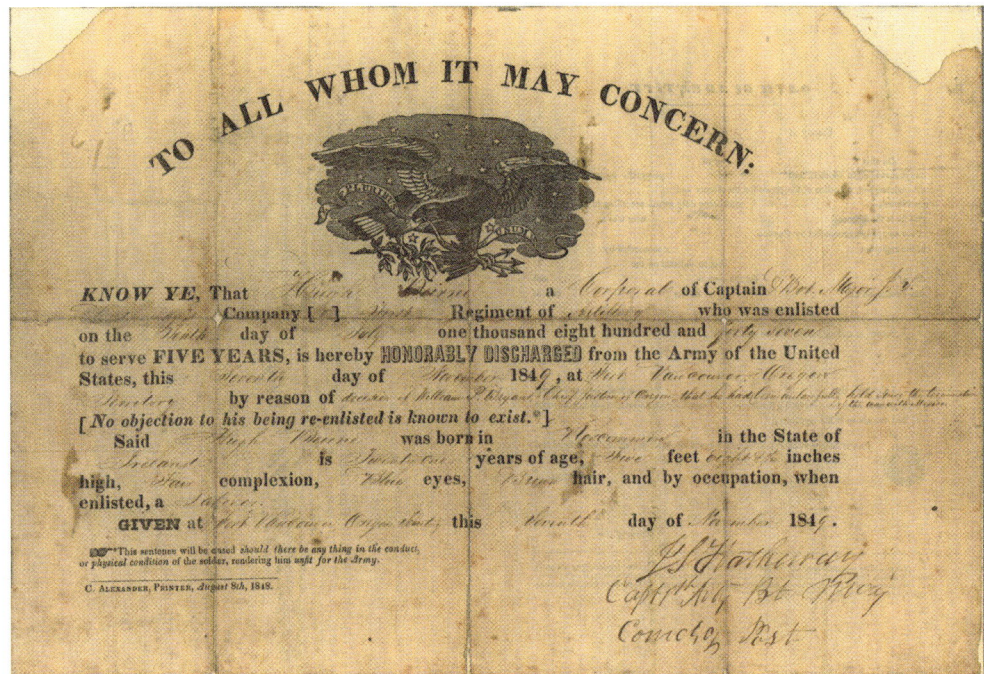

Clark County Museum

Ulysses S. Grant (1822–1885)

During the year and a half (1852–1853) Captain Grant was stationed in Vancouver as regimental quartermaster, he missed his wife, Julia, and two sons in Missouri. Grant attempted to augment his military pay with several business ventures in an effort to bring his family west. He tried shipping ice and chickens to San Francisco, hoping to sell at great profit to miners. The ice melted and the chickens died before reaching market. Next, Grant tried farming, planting a hundred acres east of the fort along the river. That spring the Columbia rose and washed away his crops. All these disastrous business ventures caused Grant to conclude that it might be better to return to Missouri and civilian life, which he did until outbreak of the Civil War.

Clark County Museum

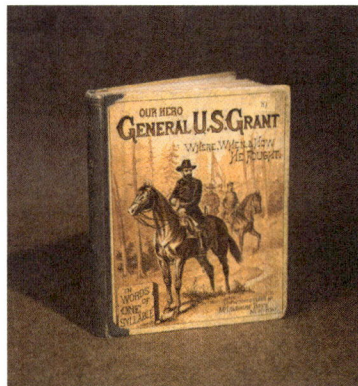

Our Hero, General U.S. Grant, **1885**

This illustrated book, "in words of one syllable," was written for "small boys, from six to twelve years of age."

Boot Scraper, Made for Lt. Phil Sheridan

Phil Sheridan served at Fort Vancouver in the 1850s, early in his military career. He was among several army officers at the barracks who later rose to fame in the army. Sheridan became a distinguished general during the Civil War, and in 1883 he became commander in chief of the U.S. Army.

The army blacksmith at Fort Yamhill made this boot scraper.

Oregon Historical Society

U.S. Army Rifle, 2nd Allin Conversion, 1866

This rifle was developed at the U.S. Arsenal in Springfield, Massachusetts, after the Civil War. During a period of sparse military funding, this weapon marked the beginning of the era of the metallic-cartridge breech loader. In an effort to economize, the army converted an enormous stock of muzzle-loading arms on hand to the quicker and more technically advanced breech-loading system.

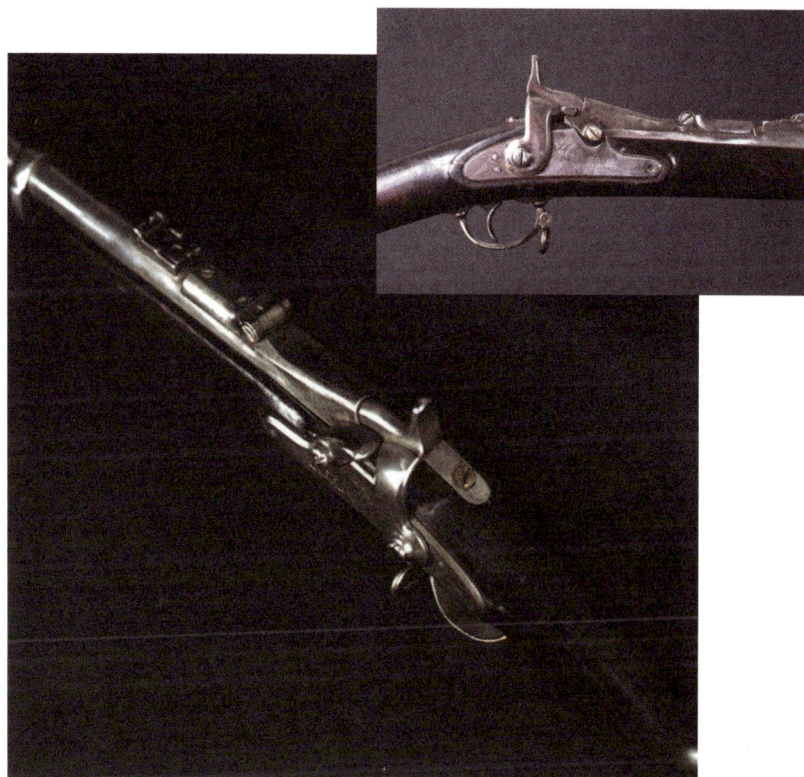

Oregon Military Museum

Fort Vancouver National Historic Site

Cannon Balls and Grape Shot

Archaeologists uncovered this ammunition used by artillery at Vancouver Barracks. The small cast-iron balls, known as a "stand of grape" for their resemblance to a cluster of grapes, are bound together to form one round of fire. Grape shot was used prior to the Civil War.

Royal Engineers Library

United States Military Post at Vancouver, 1860

The British North American Boundary Commission stopped at Fort Vancouver en route to its fieldwork at the forty-ninth parallel. The commanding officer's quarters can be seen at the right rear. This building, known as the Grant House (in honor of Ulysses S. Grant), still stands.

Clark County Museum

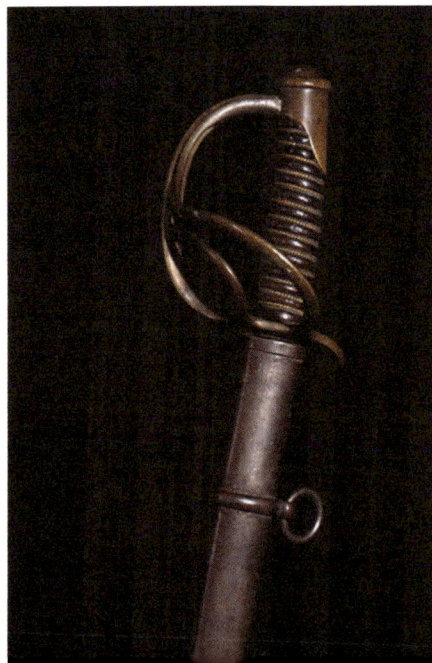

Sword, c. 1861–1865

This sword was used during the Civil War.

View of Fort Vancouver from the Northwest, 1855

by Richard Covington

This sketch shows the St. James Mission in the left foreground, the Hudson's Bay Company post and village to the right, and structures erected by the U.S. Army at the left rear.

Washington State Historical Society

Mousetrap

This device is believed to have been used at Vancouver Barracks during the nineteenth century.

Women's Work in the Civil War, 1867

This book was dedicated to "The Loyal Women of America, whose patriotic contributions, toils and sacrifices, enabled their sisters, whose history is here recorded, to minister relief and consolation to our wounded and suffering heroes." The narrative describes the Civil War activities of women in nursing and hospital work and in aid societies.

Index of General Orders, Department of the Columbia, 1866–1868 (above right)

This printed volume contains manuscripts, notes, and records from all posts and camps in the department.

81

A Clash of Cultures on the Frontier ⌒ White settlers coveted Indian lands in the West. Immigration to the region and the resulting clash of cultures changed the lives of Native groups forever. American settlement and population growth occurred at the same time the Native population drastically declined as a result of diseases brought by whites.

The Oregon Donation Land Claim Act of 1850 stimulated white settlement. Agreements and treaties between Indians and the United States were complex and resulted in misunderstandings and hostilities, causing the U.S. Army to enter the scene to police the frontier. The Nez Perce War of 1877 was one of several tragic episodes stemming from the clash of cultures.

THE ARMY AND THE NEZ PERCE INDIANS

Fort Vancouver faced a period of uncertainty during the 1860s and '70s. Department of the Columbia offices were in Portland, and the garrison force in Vancouver was reduced from former days. Troops from Fort Vancouver and other posts were called out to fight Indians in the Pacific Northwest. One of the last sad chapters in the conflict between Indians and whites was the Nez Perce War of 1877. This epic struggle of a band of Nez Perce Indians to preserve their identity, in the face of a four-month, 1400-mile pursuit by Gen. O.O. Howard and the U.S. Army, stands as an enduring American saga.

Arrival of the Nez Perce Indians at Walla Walla Treaty, May 1855
by Gustav Sohon

"Soon their cavalcade came in sight, a thousand warriors mounted fine horses and riding at a gallop, two abreast," wrote eyewitness Hazard Stevens, son of Isaac Stevens.

The Walla Walla Council was one of the largest and most heterogeneous Indian gatherings in Pacific Northwest history. Several thousand Nez Perce, Yakima, Cayuse, Walla Walla, and Palouse Indians were present. Issac Stevens, first territorial governor of Washington, organized this council and three others across eastern Washington in 1855. At Walla Walla, Indians ceded title to 45,000 square miles of land while reserving certain rights.

Engraved Elk Horn and Leather Quirt

Nez Perce horsemen used quirts as riding crops or whips. After 1805, when Lewis and Clark first encountered the tribe in its homeland between the Cascade and Rocky mountains, the Nez Perce way of life was altered. For the next seventy-five years, the Nez Perce played an important role in events surrounding the opening and early settlement of the Northwest by whites.

The horse was central to Plateau culture by the time Lewis and Clark reached the region. Introduced by the Spanish, thousands of wild horses spread north from Mexico on both sides of the Rockies, arriving in the Nez Perce homeland sometime after 1730. The tribe was noted for its skill in handling and breeding horses.

Elkhide Painted Parfleche

Indians in the interior Northwest used tanned hides to make sturdy containers for household goods. These bags were usually decorated with painted designs.

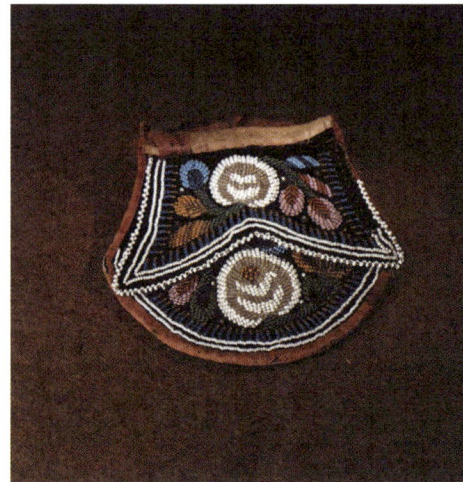

Beaded Handbag

A stylized floral design decorates this bag, which may have been obtained by the Nez Perce in trade with tribes to the east.

Beaded Pipe Bag

Nez Perce horsemen carried bags such as this.

Harper's Weekly, November 17, 1877

C.E.S. Wood traveled to Chicago after the Nez Perce War and brought sketches he had made in the field. *Harper's Weekly* interpreted these drawings and was the first to publish Chief Joseph's famous speech: "Our artist was the only person present who committed the proceedings to writing, and took the reply as it fell from the lips of the speaker. . . . Hear me, my chiefs! I am tired; my heart is sick and sad. From where the sun now stands I will fight no more forever."

C.E.S. Wood, who sympathized with the Indians, left the army in 1884 and began a successful law practice in Portland. His son Erskine, as a boy of twelve, lived with Chief Joseph for a short time in his home in Nespelem, Washington.

Charles Erskine Scott Wood (1852–1944)

Army soldier, lawyer, author, artist, and poet, C.E.S. Wood attended West Point and was General Howard's aide-de-camp during the Nez Perce War. Wood recorded Chief Joseph's famous surrender speech.

"Circling around a Wagon Train That Has Gone into Corral for Defense"

This illustration, from Major General Howard's 1907 book entitled *My Life and Experiences among Our Hostile Indians,* reflected a prevailing white view of Native Americans at the turn of the twentieth century.

Vancouver National Historic Reserve Trust

Washington State University, Museum of Anthropology, McWhorter Collection

Cartridges, Bullets from Bear Paw Mountain Battlefield

Lucullus McWhorter moved to Washington from West Virginia around 1900. He settled near the Yakima Indian Reservation and devoted the rest of his life to preserving the history of the Nez Perce and Yakima Indians. McWhorter befriended the Nez Perce and wrote two accounts of the 1877 war from the Indian perspective. Many years after the conflict, McWhorter visited the site of the battles with Yellow Wolf and Peo Peo Tholekt and collected these bullets at the Bear Paw Mountain battlefield in Montana.

Chief Joseph, Bronze Portrait Medallion, 1889

Noted New York sculptor Olin Warner modeled this portrait head while Chief Joseph was visiting C.E.S. Wood in Portland in 1889. Three medallions were cast.

Joseph's Indian name (Hinmato: wyalahtqʼit) can be translated as "Thunder Rolling in the Mountains." After the Nez Perce War, Joseph became a national symbol. The government failed to honor its promise to send the Nez Perce back to Idaho and instead shipped them to an Oklahoma reservation, where many died. Poet Robert Penn Warren wrote of the Nez Perce plight:

> "Yes, what is a piece of white paper with black
> Marks? And what is a face, white,
> With lips tight shut to hide forked tongue?"

Joseph traveled to Washington, D.C., and enlisted letters of support for the return of his people to the Northwest. Finally, in 1885, Joseph and most of his band were sent to the Colville Reservation in Washington Territory, still far from their homeland.

Oregon Historical Society

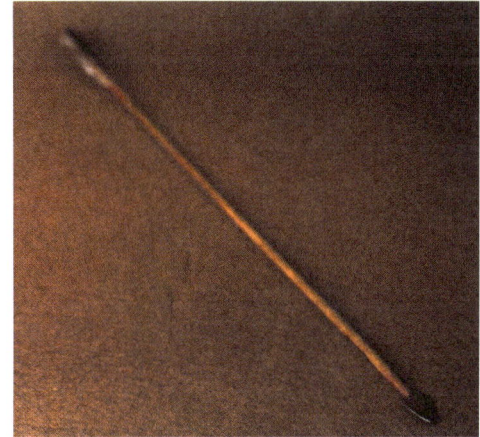

Yellow Wolf's Metal-tipped Arrow

Yellow Wolf, famed Nez Perce warrior in the 1877 war, made this arrow following the conflict and later gave it to Lucullus McWhorter. Upon McWhorter's death in 1944, his collection of artifacts was given to Washington State University in Pullman.

Chief Joseph and Gen. O.O. Howard, Carlisle, Pennsylvania, 1904

Twenty-seven years after the Nez Perce War, Joseph and Howard—former foes—met when both attended commencement exercises at Carlisle Indian School in Pennsylvania. They sat at the same banquet table and toasted each other.

Gen. O.O. Howard's Brass and Wood Coffeepot

The personal possessions of O.O. Howard, shown here were given to Howard University by the general's descendants between 1942 and 1961.

Howard used this coffeepot in the field.

General Howard's Inkwell

This portable inkwell was designed to be sealed so that ink would not spill while traveling.

Military Uniform Buttons, Hat Cord, Silk Sash, and Black-Leather Billfold Belonging to Gen. O.O. Howard

Howard wore this army-issue beige sash with double tassel as part of his dress uniform.

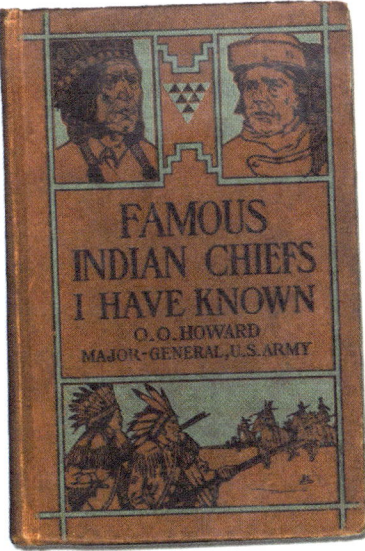

Famous Indian Chiefs I Have Known, 1907

Howard authored many books, including an autobiography. Most were written following his retirement from the military in 1894. Howard wrote and lectured to supplement his military income.

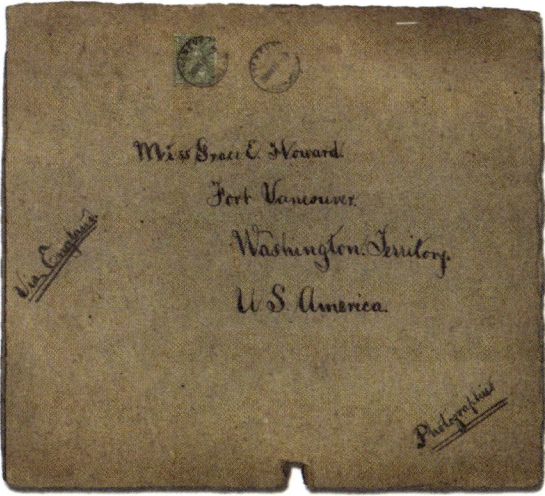

Gen. O.O. Howard Lecture Ticket and YMCA Speech Announcement

After the Civil War, General Howard began lecturing to the public. The speeches, which attracted large audiences, were on such subjects as "loyalty" and the general's military experiences.

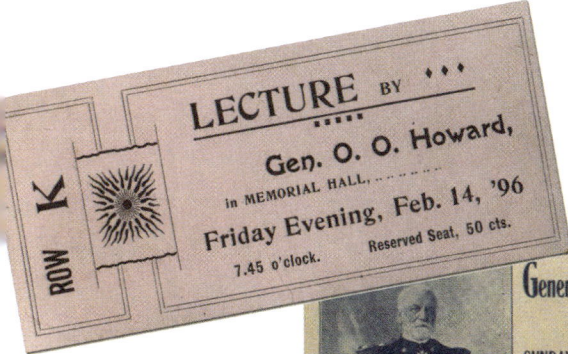

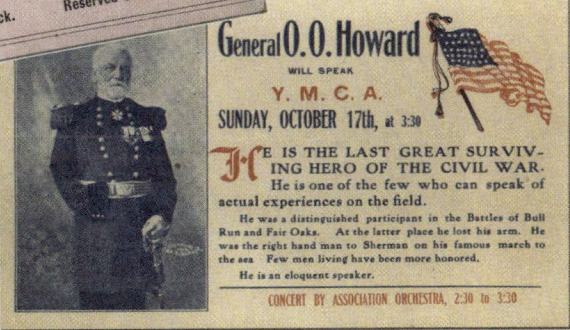

Mailing Envelope Containing Wedding Present to Grace Howard

On Wednesday evening, September 17, 1879, Grace Howard, the general's oldest daughter, was married in the west parlor of her father's residence (now known as the Howard House) at the Vancouver Barracks. Grace married local riverboat captain James T. Gray. Her descendants still live in Portland. The wedding was described by the Vancouver *Independent* as a "large and fashionable affair." The spacious rooms were "tastefully decorated for the occasion with flags, evergreens and flowers." Guests danced to the "soft strains of the regimental orchestra that was stationed in the hall." This envelope, saved by Grace Howard's family, is a tangible reminder of that long-ago evening.

AT THE MILITARY RESERVATION ∽ During the Civil War years, regular troops were sent east to serve the Union. A civilian volunteer militia ran Fort Vancouver during those years. In 1879, the post changed its name for a final time to Vancouver Barracks.

Troops in Vancouver engaged in peaceful pursuits—routine drill and target practice, work on buildings and roads, and social activities.

Officers Row, 1880s

The army constructed most of the houses along Officers Row in the 1880s. According to Gen. Nelson Miles, the garrison was "the most charming spot on the Pacific coast."

Clark County Museum

Vancouver Barracks Kitchen Interior

The recipe for a batch of "Garrison Bread" called for 100 pounds of flour. Proposals for supplies of flour requested 30,000 pounds at a time! The barracks was noted for its fine bakery. The Vancouver *Independent*, on August 2, 1877, reported: "Better bread man never eat, nor woman made, than can be found at the Post Bakery."

Clark County Museum

Manuals for Army Bakers and Cooks

Army cooks and bakers were trained in special schools. They had to know how to feed hungry soldiers in their company barracks as well as in the field.

The *Manual for Army Cooks*, published in 1910, provided thirteen ways to cook potatoes, including hashed, mashed, fried, boiled, and baked. Recipes listed such items as "Mutton Pot Pie for 609 men," which called for fifteen pounds of mutton, fifteen pounds of potatoes, three pounds of onions, two pounds of lard, and five pounds of flour.

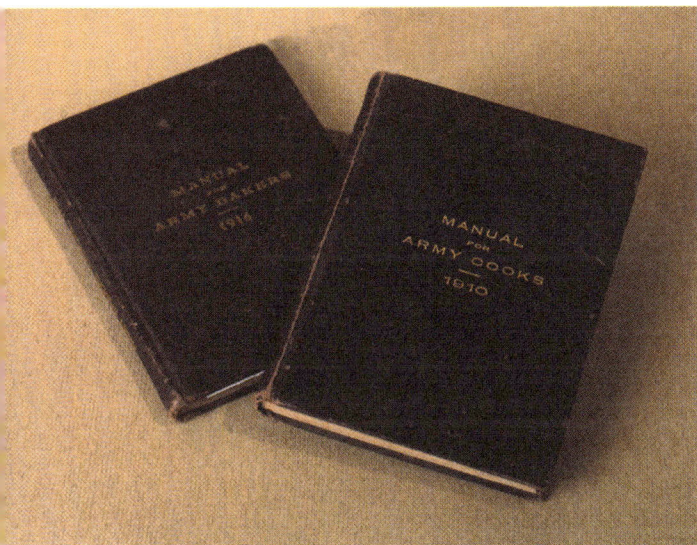

Vancouver Barracks Retiree Sub-Council

Clark County Museum

Tin Cup

This army-issue cup was found in the walls of the Grant House before the structure was refurbished in 1987.

Revolver, Patent 1878 Colt

Officers were allowed to carry civilian weapons as sidearms.

Vancouver Barracks, "Morrisy, Toby, Comiley and Two Women"

Among favorite social pastimes in the 1870s and 1880s were amateur plays by such groups as the "Sully Amateurs"—named for Post Commander Alfred Sully and performed at the Oak Grove Theatre. These "winter entertainments" received favorable reviews, and the Portland papers were "quite complimentary," the Vancouver *Independent* remarked.

In summer, croquet became the "all absorbing game in Vancouver."

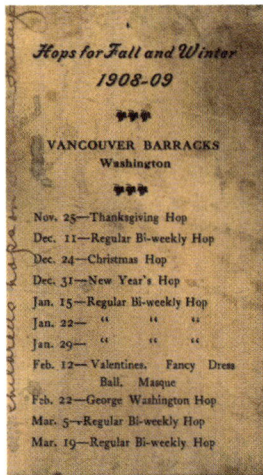

Program for Fall and Winter Hops, 1908–09

Favorite social pastimes included garrison "hops," dances to the tunes of the regimental band. The Vancouver *Independent*'s weekly "Military Items" column usually commented on the hops: "The Post 'Hop' on Tuesday evening was one of the pleasantest of the season. A number of ladies and gentlemen from Portland were in attendance."

This hop program was found in an unused fireplace at the Grant House.

Stag Pocketknife with Copper Bolster

This pocketknife, found at Fort Vancouver, could date to the Civil War. Pocketknives were popular trade items during the Hudson's Bay Company period.

Stereoscope (Patented July 28, 1903) and View Cards

Stereoscopy is the technique of generating and viewing a pair of two-dimensional images three-dimensionally. The device to view such photographs is called a "stereoscope." Special cameras with twin lenses designed in the mid-nineteenth century produced stereoscopic views, and these stereoscopes came in a variety of shapes and sizes. The popular twin pictures, called "stereoviews" or "stereographs," mounted on cardboard, were made by the millions.

In the late-nineteenth century, this entertainment device for the growing middle class was as common in the Victorian parlor as the television set is today. Special shows of the latest views toured the cities and towns of America. Vancouver was no exception. The December 9, 1880, *Independent* announced: "On Friday night of next week. . . there is to be a grand exhibition of the stereopticon at the new hall at the garrison."

Today, many organizations in the United States and abroad are devoted to the study and collection of stereography. Modern stereoscopic viewers and prints are still being made. One of the most common contemporary applications of stereoscopic photography are aerial three-dimensional images used in mapmaking.

Clark County Museum

Oregon Historical Society, neg.#24707

Vancouver Barracks

These troops posed in front of Officers Row, circa 1898. Note the troops' gear in front. A new army knapsack was invented and tested at the barracks during this period.

THE ANDERSON FAMILY ∽ Col. Thomas M. Anderson served as post commander from 1886 to 1898. He and his wife, Lizzie Van Winkle Anderson, lived with their four daughters and two sons in the post commander's quarters, now known as the Howard House. Trained as a lawyer, Anderson had a distinguished military record. Following service in the Civil War, he was stationed in Texas, Ohio, and Wyoming Territory. The Anderson family was happy to be in Vancouver, "one of the most desirable duty stations in the service," as recalled later in life by Anderson's oldest daughter, Arline.

Anderson Family, Post Commander's Residence, c. 1895

The Andersons lived in this home for twelve years, longer than any other residents. Colonel Anderson's daughter, Arline, remembered the day the family left Vancouver and "drove off down the hill to the ferry." They looked back at "the dear old house at the head of the hill," thinking that "never again would we all be together beside that fine, old fireplace listening to father telling stories."

94

Clark County Museum

Col. Thomas M. Anderson's Blick Featherweight Aluminum Typewriter, c. 1890

Colonel (later promoted to general) Anderson spent his spare time at his desk reading and writing. During the twelve years he and his family lived in the post commander's residence, his office was in the east room of the main floor. Anderson published articles in the *North American Review* and the *Oregon Historical Quarterly,* among other journals. Arline Anderson acted as his secretary and assisted with typing chores. Anderson's descendants still live in Vancouver.

Christine Donaugh and Beth Gilbert

Chin Wing, the Andersons' Cantonese Cook, c. 1890

Officers kept servants and often employed Chinese cooks. Chin Wing worked for the Andersons for eleven years, serving as "Chinese cook supreme," housekeeper, household bookkeeper, and laundry man.

"Nannie with Her Charges," Vancouver Barracks

Officers and their families lived a privileged life in the last decades of the nineteenth century, with servants to handle daily chores.

Clark County Museum

"One of the Roads in the Reservation back of Vancouver Barracks," Known as the "North Woods," c. 1897

Left to right, Arline Anderson, Mrs. Anderson, and Bess Anderson. Arline wrote of the setting: "Back of the garrison there still remained a . . . forest primeval. Into this wood we walked almost daily."

Silver-plate Teaspoon, Used by Col. Thomas M. Anderson

Many social activities took place on Officers Row during Anderson's tenure as post commander. Chief Joseph visited Gen. John Gibbon at Vancouver Barracks in 1889. General Gibbon, who had commanded the army at the Big Hole battle during the 1877 Nez Perce War, hosted a lunch party for Joseph, which the Andersons attended. Gibbon at that time lived in the quarters for the commander of the Department of the Columbia, now known as the Marshall House, on Officers Row.

Shortly before World War I, the army reorganized and abolished the Department of the Columbia.

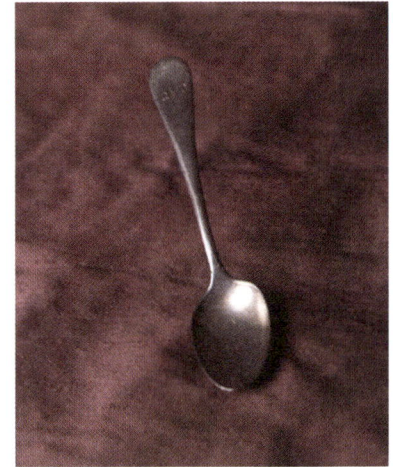

Vancouver National Historic Reserve Trust

Clark County Museum

Col. Thomas M. Anderson's Dress-Uniform Hat

This chapeau-style hat evolved from eighteenth-century military design and was in use by the U.S. Army from the early 1800s until World War I. Officially, its use was allowed until shortly before World War II.

GARRISON LIFE AT THE TURN OF THE CENTURY ⬦ The year 1900 was a time of relative peace, when the dawn of a new century marked a spirit of optimism. The transition of the Portland/Vancouver area from frontier outpost to sophisticated metropolis was under way.

Life appeared good to the officers and their families living at Vancouver Barracks during this time. With servants to do daily housework, picnics, regimental band concerts, "hops," and plays were all regular features of social life.

Vancouver Barracks, Looking West during High Water, 1887

The building in the foreground is a guardhouse. The fenced structure to the right of the guardhouse is a cistern. In the distance, post headquarters and a flagpole can be seen on the parade grounds to the right. Today, the Fort Vancouver National Historic Site Visitor Center is located in the same vicinity.

National Archives

97

Clark County Museum

Band Concert, Vancouver Barracks Parade Ground

According to Col. George Van Way, the highly skilled regimental band was respected as an "essential element of the command." The Vancouver *Independent* of June 28, 1877, reported: "The Band gives a free serenade every day at six o'clock, Saturdays excepted."

Clark County Museum

Sgt. Joseph White, Bandleader, 1913

Many African Americans served at Vancouver Barracks. Among them was Sgt. Joseph White and First Sgt. Moses Williams, who received the Medal of Honor for his service in an 1881 Indian campaign along the Texas–New Mexico border. Williams was a member of the Ninth Cavalry Regiment, which fought in the West after the Civil War. Williams died at Vancouver Barracks in 1899 and is buried in the Post Cemetery.

The Ninth and Tenth Cavalry regiments were known as "Buffalo Soldiers," a name bestowed upon them by their Indian foes.

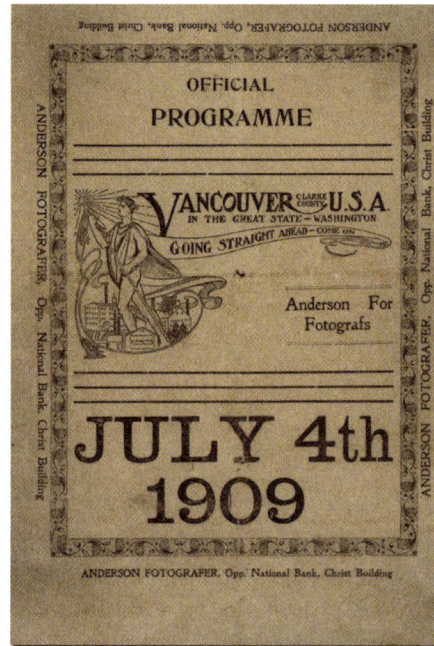

OFFICIAL PROGRAMME

VANCOUVER CLARKE COUNTY U.S.A.
IN THE GREAT STATE — WASHINGTON
GOING STRAIGHT AHEAD — COME ON?

Anderson For Fotografs

ANDERSON FOTOGRAFER, Opp. National Bank, Christ Building

JULY 4th 1909

Vancouver, July 4th Program, 1909

July 4th celebrations have been a staple in the Vancouver community since the 1870s. Fireworks "of all kinds" were advertised for sale in the Vancouver *Independent* in 1878. "A grand display of fireworks" took place every year, usually in City Park, which is "universally admitted to be the most beautiful Park on the Northwest Coast." The Infantry Band provided the music at these celebrations.

Jim Raley Collection

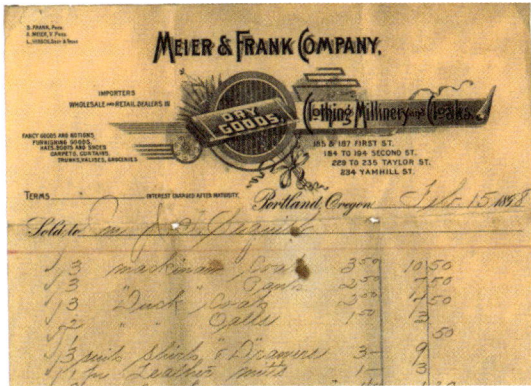

Receipt from Meier & Frank Department Store for Supplies Taken to Alaska

The year 1898 was a busy one at Vancouver Barracks. Gen. Thomas Anderson and the Fourteenth Infantry were ordered north during the Alaska gold rush to guard Chilkoot Pass, the route to the goldfields. The Fourteenth Infantry Regiment served at Vancouver Barracks on four different occasions prior to World War I.

The Fourteenth, along with the Seventh and Twenty-First infantries, were the longest-serving regiments at Vancouver Barracks.

Spanish-American War, Philippines, Cpl. William M. Pearson, Seated, and Sgt. Willis A. Gott, Company H, First Washington Infantry

Vancouver Barracks played an important role in the mobilization and training of troops for the Spanish-American War. This brief conflict between the United States and Spain took place between April and August 1898. In May, troops from Vancouver were ordered to the Philippines, with General Anderson in charge.

These two soldiers had their photograph taken while stationed in Manila. The Spanish-American War marked America's emergence as a power in the international arena.

Undine, Portland-to-Vancouver Ferry, 1909

This photo was taken on the day the soldiers at Vancouver went on parade for Pres. William Howard Taft's Portland visit. The sternwheeler *Undine* maintained connections between Portland and Vancouver for thirty-four years, from 1888 to 1922.

Brass Collar Disks

These disks were excavated at Fort Vancouver and likely date to the period shortly after World War I. Soldiers wore these insignia on their collars to designate regiment and branch of service.

AT VANCOUVER DEPOT ⟿ Soldiers from the barracks went on field maneuvers to such places as "Tigardville" and Camp Bonneville, marching and camping along the way. They visited Portland's Lewis and Clark Fair in 1905 and Seattle's Alaska-Yukon-Pacific Exposition in 1909. Both these fairs brought population growth to the region. When visitors came to see the sights, they often decided to stay.

"At Ease," Eighth Infantry, Vancouver Barracks

Soldiers filled their bed sacks with fresh hay or straw.

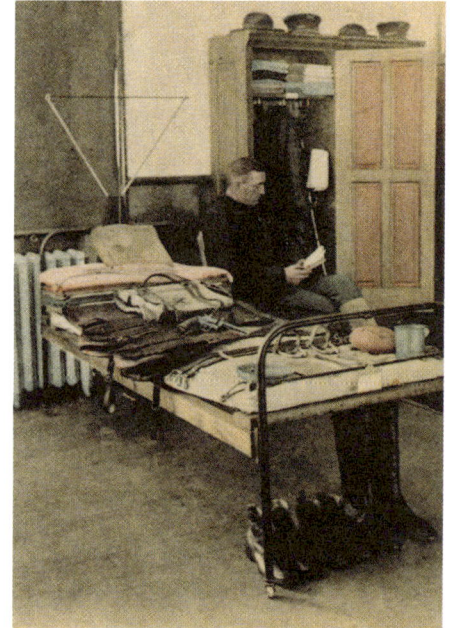

Private Collection

Jim Raley Collection

Post Commander's Quarters, c. 1910

Mules and horses were an important part of the military routine. The army relied on mules to carry supplies at Vancouver Barracks until after World War II. A mule barn, which now houses office workers, still stands on the reserve.

Soldier with Bugle

"Taps" dates from the Civil War. The playing of this melodious bugle call was eventually written into U.S. Army regulations.

Vancouver resident Bill Moore remembered: "When I was growing up I lived on Eleventh Street. Every night at ten o'clock, they'd play taps up in the barracks, and at each end of the Post they had these two megaphones, and I'd be lying in my bed, and I'd listen to them play taps."

Oregon Historical Society, neg.#90964

Clark County Museum

Reservoir at Vancouver Barracks, c. 1890

The garrison had its own water system, with the reservoir located in the northern part of the military reservation.

The Vancouver *Independent* reported on August 15, 1878, that "3,000 feet of two inch iron water pipe arrived yesterday . . . to increase the water supply."

Fort Vancouver National Historic Site

Bugle

Bugles were communication and signal devices, played by army trumpeters both in the field and at the garrison.

Officers at Vancouver Barracks

Charles Martin, seated on the far right, was assigned to Vancouver Barracks in 1887. Martin knew George Marshall from their service together in the Far East. Martin and Marshall renewed their friendship in the 1930s, while Marshall was stationed in Vancouver and Martin was governor of Oregon.

Oregon Historical Society, neg.#98848

THE GOVERNMENT RESERVATION 🙢

Vancouver Barracks has been variously known as the "Post," the "Depot," the "Government Reservation," and the "Barracks." Today, people often mistakenly refer to the barracks as "Fort Vancouver"—the name of the old Hudson's Bay Company post.

Vancouver Barracks, Artillery Practice, 1909

Artillery and rifle practice were part of a soldier's routine.

Clark County Museum

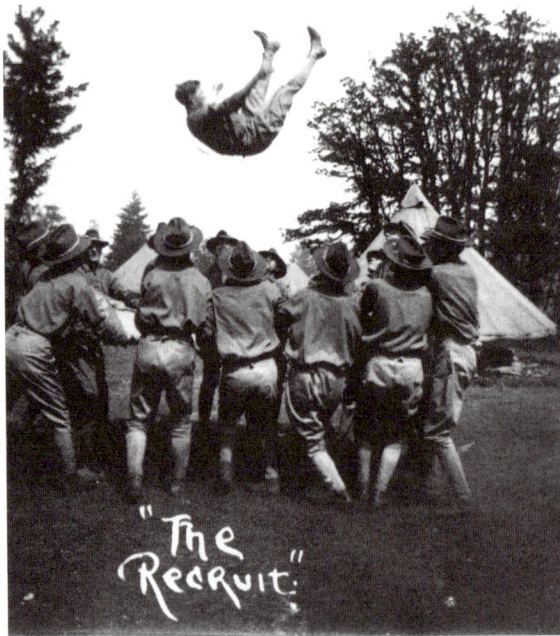

Jim Raley Collection

"The Recruit," 1909 Postcard

The troops shown here are breaking in a new soldier in military tradition with tricks and games.

Vancouver Barracks, c. 1880

The troops are conducting a "team building" exercise, in which members rely on each other to reach the specified goal. Such exercises continue to be part of confidence-building courses.

Clark County Museum

Post Exchange, c. 1900

Col. Henry A. Morrow inaugurated the U.S. Army post exchange, or PX, system at Vancouver Barracks in 1880. Originally set up as a "canteen," or simply a place to go for refreshment other than to nearby saloons, the idea soon spread to various western posts.

Canteen Token, Vancouver Barracks

Tokens were used in the barracks canteen to purchase items.

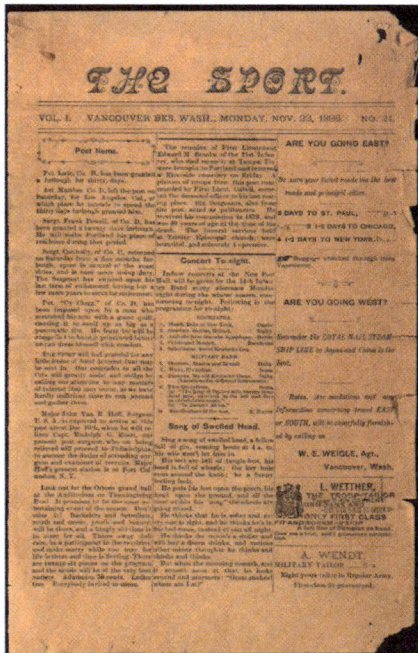

The *Sport* Newsletter, Vancouver Barracks, November 23, 1896

This regimental paper began publication in 1894 and is likely the first example of such an army barracks newsletter.

Log Cabin Saloon, c. 1910

"Tuesday was pay day at the Post, and since then sprees have been in order among some of the soldiers," the Vancouver *Independent* remarked on May 20, 1876. Numerous saloons lined the streets of Vancouver, catering to the army's thirst.

Several breweries also located in nineteenth-century Vancouver, among them Henry Weinhard, Anton Young, Star, and Columbia.

Officers Row, c. 1910

Concrete sidewalks were a recent improvement at the barracks when this color postcard was made.

A NEW CENTURY ～ At the beginning of the twentieth century, average pay for a nonofficer was thirteen dollars per month, with twenty-five cents taken out to support the Old Soldiers Home. Each company (about a hundred men) had its own mess, dayroom, and sleeping area. Rifle practice and sports played a big part in the routine.

Post Identification Pass, Vancouver Barracks

The general public was not allowed access to the military reservation. Guards were posted at the entrance gates, and a pass was required from everyone seeking entrance to the post.

Guarded Entrance to Vancouver Barracks, 1897

The sign reads, "Dogs, Fast Driving, Eating Lunches, Bicycles, Sidewalks, Carriages Not Allowed."

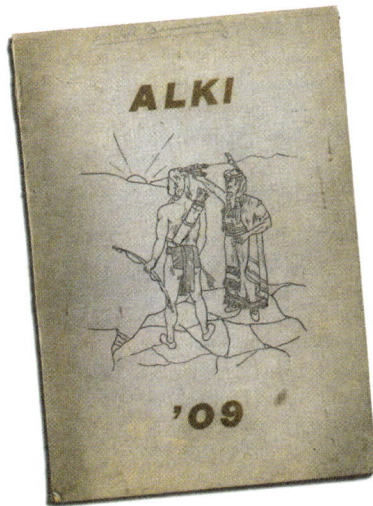
Clark County Museum

Alki, Vancouver High School 1909 Yearbook

Vancouver's first public high school was established in 1888. It was one of only six in the state when Washington was admitted to the Union in 1889.

On the March, "Vancouver or Bust," 1909

Moving troops away from their base was an elaborate operation, providing valuable lessons in planning, adapting to different terrain, logistical support (delivery of supplies), and communications. Marching kept soldiers in good physical condition.

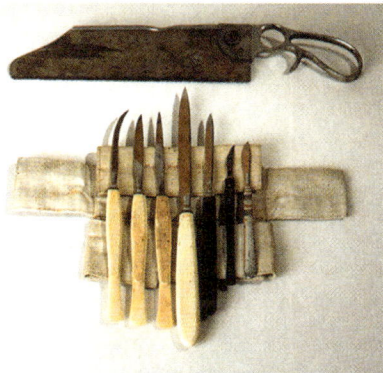

Surgical Kit and Saw

These medical tools belonged to Dr. Randolph G. Ebert, who was stationed at Vancouver Barracks and served in the Spanish-American War.

Vancouver Barracks Retiree Sub-Council

Soap, Mount Hood Soap Company

The Quartermaster Department was in charge of ordering everyday supplies such as this bar of soap, manufactured by a company now long gone.

Vancouver Barracks Retiree Sub-Council

Vancouver's Franklin School, c. 1915

In 1879 a school for the instruction of officers' and soldiers' children opened at the garrison. The following year, a new building was erected as the post school. Later, children of military personnel attended local schools.

This photo shows students diagraming sentences, with an ageless adage on the chalkboard.

"Slim, Mizner, Park, and Parson," at Vancouver Barracks, c. 1917

Army recruits pose for the camera prior to the First World War. Noble Mizner (second from left), from Camas, Washington, died in the war.

Note the canvas leggings, which formed a standard part of enlisted men's uniforms when breeches were worn. Canvas leggings, called "mud catchers," proved unsuitable in the trenches of France. Gen. John Pershing, U.S. commanding general in World War I, recommended that the men wear wrapped woolen leggings. Light and flexible, warm and easily cleaned, they were immediately popular with the troops.

Vancouver National Historic Reserve Trust

Holiday Menus and Napkin

Special menus were printed at Thanksgiving and Christmas. Companies competed with each other at such times in providing good meals. The *Manual for Army Cooks* spelled out menus for holiday dinners.

Postcards, Vancouver, c. 1910–20

Postcards served important communication needs in the days before household telephones were common. At the turn of the twentieth century, most communities had their own set of postal views, and Vancouver was no exception.

The troops at the barracks sent brief newsy messages to the folks at home, or one could send a quick note across town to Great-Aunt Bertha announcing your Wednesday afternoon visit.

Historical postcards transport one to an earlier time. It is easy to appreciate why they are enjoyed today as a popular nostalgia collectible.

Vancouver National Historic Reserve Trust

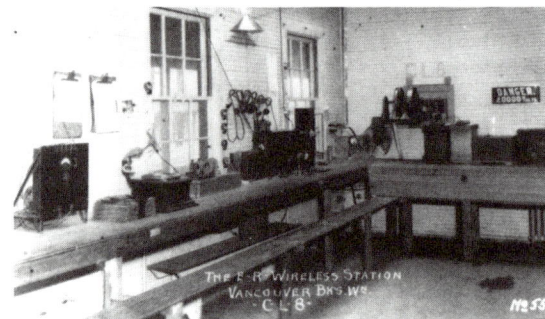

Wireless Station, Vancouver Barracks, c. 1905

The urgent need for communications in the military has helped advance technology—from the earliest telephones to today's cell phones.

"OVER THERE" ⁓ When the United States entered World War I in 1917, Vancouver Barracks became an important recruitment center. Troop trains leaving from Vancouver shipped men and women out for overseas duty. During "the war to end all wars," government nurses came to work in the enlarged post hospital. The worldwide flu epidemic arrived in Vancouver.

Vancouver National Historic Reserve Trust

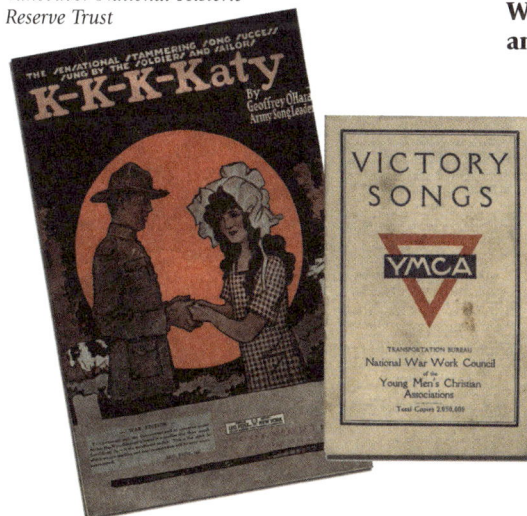

World War I–Era Sheet Music and YMCA Songbook

Lively songs recall this time in our nation's history. Many women served in France in YMCA-operated canteens catering to soldiers fighting at the front.

Vancouver National Historic Reserve Trust, Sherry Mowatt Collection

Army Signal Corps, "Hello Girls" Telephone Operators, Souilly, France, 1918

More than 40,000 women served the United States during the Great War in relief and military duty—in the army, navy, marines, Signal Corps, Red Cross, Salvation Army, and YMCA.

Women across the nation, including fourteen from Washington state, enlisted for overseas duty as French-speaking telephone operators with the Signal Corps. Nicknamed "Hello Girls," they provided an important link in vital communications at the front. Many were college students, recruited from newspaper announcements. More than 7,600 applied. Two hundred twenty-three made the cut and were sent abroad.

Jennie Young Selby (first row, second from right) enlisted from the University of Washington and likely passed through the Vancouver garrison on her way to France.

U.S. Army Ninety-first Infantry Division Jacket

While many soldiers from Oregon and Washington fought in France, others served on the home front. The January 1, 1918, *Oregonian* noted: "When history shall have been written it will be realized how stupendous a part the axes and mills of the Pacific Northwest played in winning the war for democracy."

Campaign Hat

Campaign hats were a standard part of the army uniform from at least the Spanish-American War to World War II.

Roll of Khaki Wool for Leggings (lower right)

Spiral-wound leggings, or puttees (from the Hindustani word for bandage or strip of cloth), formed a gaiter, covering the lower leg. Vancouver resident Warren Castrey recalled: "We had wrapped leggings back then. You had to start at the ankle and wind around."

During the war, the Vancouver Woolen Mills, a branch of the Washougal plant, made khaki and gray yarn. Blankets were also manufactured at Washougal.

Oregon Historical Society and Fort Vancouver National Historic Site (hat)

Vancouver Barracks Retiree Sub-Council

What Sammy's Doing: Being a Pictorial Sketch of the Soldier's Life, 1917

Before a recruit "went across" to France, booklets such as this were designed to acquaint him with everyday life.

Nurses, Vancouver Barracks, c. 1918

The first "government nurses" arrived in Vancouver in February 1918. The post hospital was then enlarged from 100 to 150 beds. The Red Cross erected a building across from the hospital, and local women volunteered for wrapping bandages and making dressings from sphagnum moss.

On August 10, 1918, under the heading "Three Hundred Moss Pads Needed at Post Hospital," the Vancouver *Daily Columbian* reported: "The ladies of Vancouver are especially urged to turn out in large numbers . . . to make moss pads for the base hospital at Vancouver Barracks."

Departing by Train, Vancouver Barracks

The military used special trains to transport the troops to war. According to the Vancouver *Daily Columbian*, on July 22, 1918: "The women of the Red Cross will provide each soldier with a box lunch as dining service on the train is limited."

Letters from France

Pvt. Otto Hazel wrote these letters to his sweetheart, Marie Bodley.

Military Funeral at Vancouver Barracks

The worldwide Spanish influenza epidemic hit Vancouver in the fall of 1918. All activities at the post were shut down. Schools were closed, and there were no public gatherings. Everyone was required to wear gauze masks.

Warren Castrey recalled that he "saw eleven funerals in one day. The band played for them. . . . They marched them up Reserve Street . . . to the military cemetery."

"GET OUT THE SPRUCE" ⌒ During World War I, one of the world's largest sawmills operated at Vancouver Barracks, on the site of the Hudson's Bay Company depot. The cut-up plant, run by the U.S. Army, supplied straight-grained spruce for airplane production. Spruce was an essential material because it was lightweight and strong. The army located the mill in Vancouver because the town hosted a regional military headquarters and was close to large supplies of coastal spruce. The railroad had reached Vancouver, providing a ready transportation link to East coast airplane production plants.

"Spruce for the Air, Fir for the Sea," Loyal Legion of Loggers and Lumbermen

This poster became a symbol for the Spruce Production Division of the Army Signal Corps, and for the government-sponsored labor organization known as the 4-Ls, or Loyal Legion of Loggers and Lumbermen.

Clark County Museum

Spruce Production Plant, Vancouver Barracks, 1918

About 30,000 soldiers were involved in all aspects of spruce production. At Vancouver, they were housed in tents in the cantonment (temporary troop quarters) adjacent to the mill. Vancouver schoolchildren donated flowers to make the soldiers' surroundings more attractive. The spruce mill was identified by a twelve-foot-high electric sign— "Vancouver Spruce Cut-up Plant"—which was illuminated at night. The plant itself was protected by a double line of guards and a great battery of searchlights.

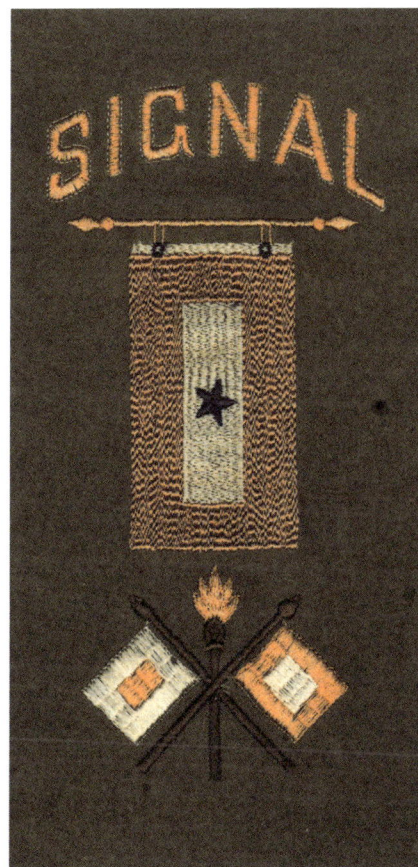

Sam Jones Collection

Signal Corps Banner (6"x12")

Mothers hung small banners in their homes to show they had sons in the military.

111

SPRUCE SQUADRONS AND THE GREAT WAR ~ Air power pushed the grassy fields of Vancouver Barracks into national prominence when the United States entered World War I. In only forty-five days, the site of the former Hudson's Bay Company depot was transformed into the world's largest spruce cut-up plant, providing lumber for the Allies' airplane production. The U.S. Army Signal Corps was in charge of the fifty-acre cut-up mill. All aspects of spruce production employed a workforce of approximately 30,000 men.

Bill Farr Collection

Loyal Legion of Loggers and Lumbermen Membership Button

The 4-Ls was a labor organization formed by Signal Corps officers to increase spruce production during World War I. Its members worked on behalf of the nation's defense.

The Portland *Oregonian* of January 1, 1918, explained that the government button showed "an airplane hovering over a ship at sea, between two trees, being symbolical of the forest supply and its two urgent war uses. It bears the initials of the legion and the authorization of the Secretary of War, also the device of a crossed saw and ax between the letters U.S."

Spruce Cut-up Mill Opening Ceremonies, "Spruce Will Win the War," February 7, 1918

Six-thousand soldiers and civilians joined in celebrating the opening of the spruce mill in Vancouver. The plant was built in a remarkable month-and-a-half and cost $250,000. Production of lumber for airplane spruce increased to 1 million board feet a day.

Clark County Museum

Straight Grain Newspaper, Vancouver Barracks

The *Straight Grain* was the official publication of the entire post. The newspaper, delivered to all the tents, was published from October 26, 1918, until January 4, 1919.

The *Straight Grain* announced in an early issue that "the greater part of the paper will consist of things the soldiers have written and drawn themselves." The paper also included jokes, such as the following:

> "A line of Rookies edged up to the sergeant for assignment—
>
> 'I am a lawyer.'
> 'Go to the regimental supply office and start opening cases.'
>
> 'My name is Percival Perkins, college graduate, Ph.D., A.B.M.D.Lt.D.'
> 'Well seeing as you are such a man of letters, you can act as mail orderly.'"

"Sprucers" in the Washington Woods, 1918
by Asahel Curtis

In January 1918, 4-L "soldier-loggers" won the eight-hour day and time-and-a-half pay for overtime work. Working conditions in the woods improved during the national war emergency.

"So Long, Old Mill! We've Done Our Stretch," *Straight Grain* Newspaper

As operations at the mill ceased, a cartoon in the December 21, 1918, issue expressed the troops' mixed feelings as they departed Vancouver— glad to go home, but proud to have done their part for the war effort.

IWW "Stickerettes"

The Industrial Workers of the World (IWW), a national labor union formed in 1905, advocated fair wages, an eight-hour day, and safe working conditions. This group, also known as the Wobblies, found support in the Northwest timber industry. The period from 1917 to 1919 was marked by violence and strikes, particularly in Washington. These stickers helped promote the IWW.

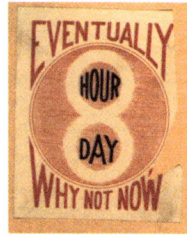

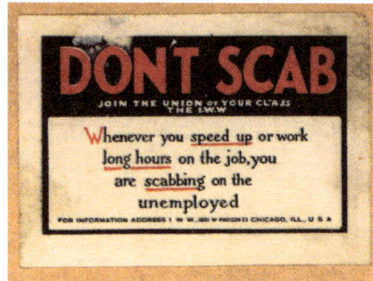

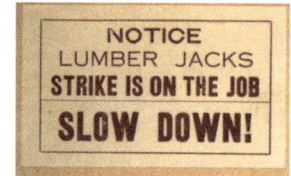

Bill Farr Collection

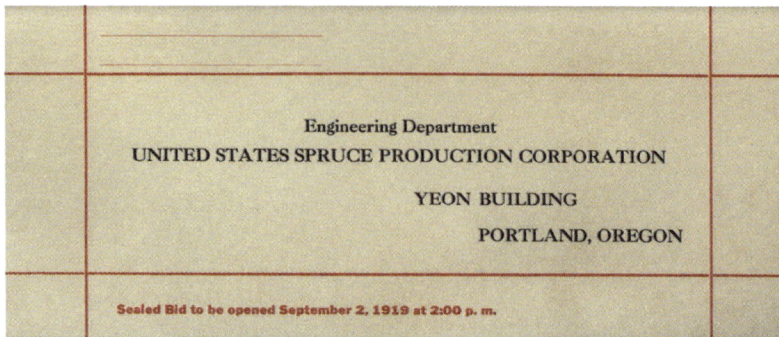

Bid Envelope, Spruce Production Corporation Property Sale

Fort Vancouver National Historic Site

When the war ended, the cut-up mill at Vancouver Barracks had more than 4 million feet of airplane lumber ready for shipment. Eight hundred soldiers inventoried and stored the leftover material. The Spruce Division formed a sales board to market all major materials and equipment through sealed bid. Brice Disque, commander of the Spruce Production Division, claimed that the effort represented "the largest sale of Government property ever advertised, only the sale of equipment from the Panama Canal excelling it in number of items and valuation." The U.S. Spruce Production Corporation still existed in 1946, with four employees.

Liberty Bond Parade, Vancouver

The Vancouver community supported the war effort with Liberty Bond drives. Local theaters played such movies as *The Kaiser* and *Pershing's Crusaders.* The Hazelwood Restaurant offered ice-cream treats with names such as "Flying Ace," "Over the Top," and "The Aviation." Volunteers knitted sweaters and socks for the soldiers.

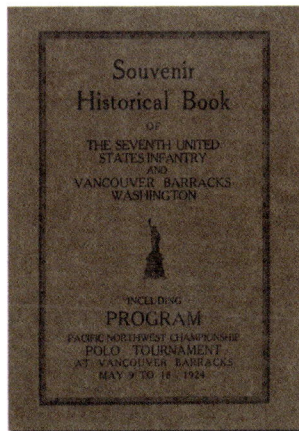

Vancouver National Historic Reserve Trust

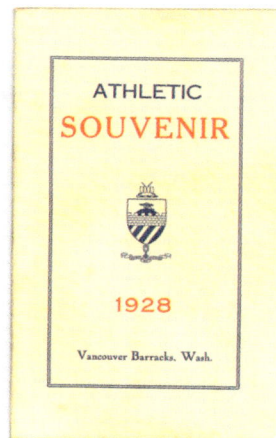

Clark County Museum

Souvenir Booklets, Vancouver Barracks, 1924 and 1928

These two printed programs for athletic competitions show the value the army placed on sporting events and physical fitness. After World War I, polo again became a popular pastime at the barracks. Members of the Seventh Infantry polo team were both Washington and Pacific Northwest champions in 1924.

BETWEEN THE WORLD WARS: GEORGE MARSHALL AND THE CCC

Congress created the Civilian Conservation Corps (CCC) in 1933. The corps represented both a federal response to the Depression and a renewal of thoughtful stewardship of our nation's natural resources—a commitment that had waned since the days of U.S. Forest Service chief Gifford Pinchot and Pres. Theodore Roosevelt. Pres. Franklin D. Roosevelt's purpose in establishing the CCC was to provide employment for young men and to put the enrollees to work on conservation projects. During its nine-year life, more than 3 million men served in "3C" camps in every state of the Union.

Gen. George C. Marshall (1880–1959)
by Dale Denny

Brig. Gen. George Marshall arrived at Vancouver Barracks in 1936, his first command post as a new general. He thoroughly enjoyed his two-year stay in Vancouver, intrigued by the historic character of the western outpost and the scenic beauty of the area.

Marshall considered supervision of the CCC camps his most important job. He called the CCC the "most instructive service I have ever had, and the most interesting." Feeding, clothing, housing, transporting, and educating thousands of enrollees required a massive organizational effort.

China Plate, Coffee Cup, and Fork, CCC Camps, Columbia National Forest

These eating utensils from Camp Hemlock and Twin Buttes helped keep the "boys" well fed. The crockery is similar to that used in most Northwest logging camps in the first part of the twentieth century. "CCC Camp 944" is stamped on the fork, indicating that it belonged to Camp Hemlock.

Gifford Pinchot National Forest

Gifford Pinchot National Forest

CCC Canteen, Blazing Ax, and Saw-Oil Bottle

The CCC taught discipline and teamwork to those who worked and lived together in the woods. The regular army quartermaster at Vancouver Barracks supplied the CCC camps, a task he took on in addition to his usual work. In a five-year period, among other achievements, the quartermaster saw to the repair of some 80,000 pairs of shoes. Laundry services amounted to approximately $325,000. The Vancouver Barracks district finance office had disbursed more than $43 million by 1938.

Mess Line, CCC Camp, Washington

In 1933, Vancouver Barracks became district headquarters for the Ninth Corps Area Civilian Conservation Corps. The district encompassed 44,000 square miles and twenty-seven outlying camps in Oregon and southern Washington.

Meals were the pride of the CCC. One of the enrollees remarked: "We eat good, by golly."

CCC Survey Crew

Sometimes called "Roosevelt's Tree Army," the CCC had about five applicants for each opening. The young men, mostly eighteen or nineteen years old, were paid thirty dollars a month and frequently sent money home to their families. Marshall started a semimonthly newspaper, the *Review*, to facilitate communication among the camps and to boost morale.

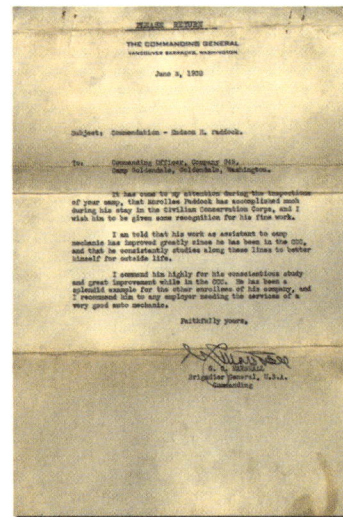

Picnic Area, Recreational Forest Camp Built by the 3C's

CCC operations ran under the cooperative management of several federal agencies—the Departments of Labor, War, Agriculture, and Interior. As one official put it, "The Forest Service took care of the boys during the day and the Army took over at night."

The "Tree Troopers" brought lasting changes to the Pacific Northwest woods. The "boys" built campgrounds, roads, trails, bridges, and forest-fire lookouts. They fought fires, planted trees, and strung phone lines, creating an enduring legacy in the region's forestlands.

CCC Letter of Commendation

George Marshall started a recognition program for the CCC, writing letters of commendation to outstanding enrollees in the Vancouver district.

Marshall and his men shared warm feelings of mutual regard and respect. When Marshall left for Washington, editors of the CCC *Review* published many of the hundreds of letters that poured in paying tribute to their leader. A cartoon from the June 1, 1938, issue depicted Marshall driving off to Washington with a letter of commendation from his charges: "We know you always placed our welfare first. Signed: Enrollees of Vancouver CCC District."

PREFACE TO A HEROIC CAREER ~ Gen. George Marshall brought energy and enthusiasm to Vancouver. After a lifetime in the military, Marshall's responsibilities gave his management and diplomatic skills a chance to bloom in the Northwest. Prior to leaving Vancouver, he was considering retirement. In preparation, he and his wife, Katherine, had even selected a choice-view lot.

World events interrupted his plans, and Marshall instead accepted assignment to the War Department in Washington, D.C. Within a year, President Roosevelt selected Marshall for his new army chief of staff. After the war ended in 1945, George Marshall drew up a plan for economic recovery for war-torn Europe, later known as the Marshall Plan. Marshall possessed an extraordinary intellect, an astounding memory, and a genius for organization. He served as both secretary of state and secretary of defense. In 1953, he was awarded the Nobel Peace Prize.

CCC Patch, Camp Goldendale, Company 945

More than 40,000 young men, coming from every state in the nation, had served in the CCC Vancouver Barracks district (Ninth Corps area) by 1937. The United States was organized into nine geographic-administrative areas, and camp numbers indicated a camp's location.

CCC Sunset Camp, Columbia National Forest (Now Gifford Pinchot National Forest)

While federal land-management agencies identified worthwhile projects for the CCC, the army was able to organize these large groups of men quickly and to care for their basic needs. The army provided camps with recreation halls, organized sports competitions between camps, put on dances, and allowed weekend passes.

Marshall sought to encourage the educational mission of the CCC. The program, which offered opportunities to learn trades or marketable skills, prepared enrollees for work in civilian life. Seventy different jobs were identified for the Vancouver district. Many young men learned to read and write, and then finished high school while in the CCC.

Marshall made frequent inspection trips to the remote camps. His wife, Katherine, often accompanied him on these trips and joined him fishing. She later recalled fondly, "We spent many days together in that magnificent country."

Vancouver Barracks Library

The post had offered a library for the troops since the nineteenth century. The CCC camps also provided libraries with comfortable chairs and reading tables.

CCC Patch

This rare CCC shoulder uniform patch depicts the natural resources—trees, water, and land—with which the organization worked.

Vancouver National Historic Reserve Trust

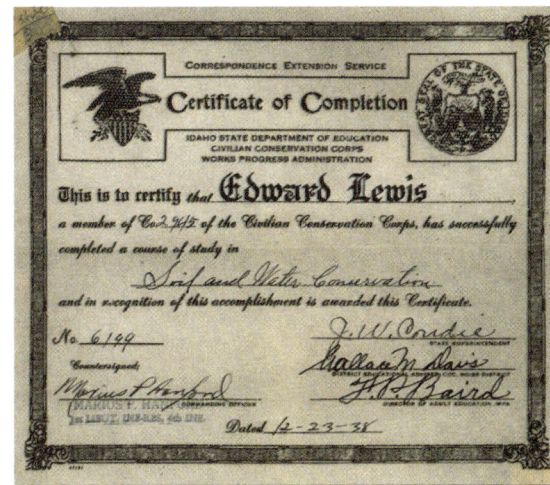

CCC Matchbook Covers

Matchcovers were a popular advertising form, promoting every aspect of America, from beer and cigarettes to the military and movies. More than 500 different CCC matchcovers are known, dating from 1933 to 1942.

CCC Certificate of Completion

Instructors provided training to CCC enrollees in a variety of subjects, such as soil and water conservation.

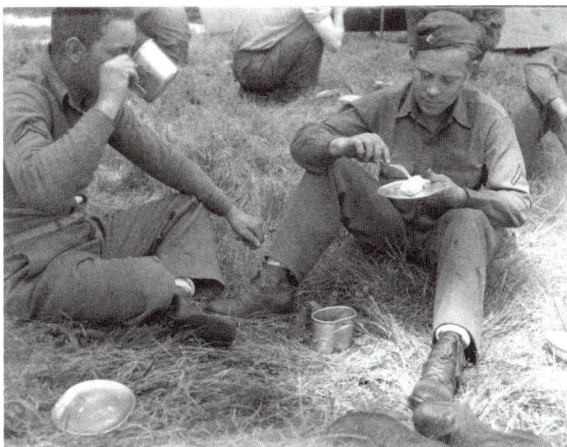

Vancouver National Historic Reserve Trust, Dale Denny Collection

Vancouver Barracks

by Dale Denny

Another national civilian program for youth, started after World War I, was the Citizens Military Training Camps (CMTC). The agency was formally recognized by the U.S. Army, and camps were organized under provisions of the National Defense Act of 1920.

The program's purpose was to provide voluntary military training for young men between the ages of seventeen and twenty-five. Vancouver Barracks ran monthlong summer training camps for the CMTC. The campers lived in the cantonment area north of Officers Row, where the "Sprucers" had lived earlier. George Marshall trained young men at CMTC camps during his military career.

CHAPTER FOUR
PEARSON FIELD

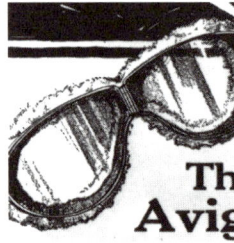

the Wright brothers made aviation history on the
windy dunes of Kitty Hawk, North Carolina,
daring young "birdmen" began defying gravity
on the open fields of Vancouver Barracks. The
broad riverfront was a popular location for
the region's first attempts at flight. Aerial
adventurers attempted incredible stunts—
including flying from the roof of a downtown
Portland hotel.

Oregon Historical Society, neg.#24279

Silas Christofferson, Multnomah Hotel Rooftop, June 12, 1912

A crowd of 50,000 gathered to watch
Silas Christofferson fly from a specially
built runway atop the new Multnomah
Hotel to what many thought would be
his doom. Christofferson, an ex–
automobile racer, taught himself to fly
and built his own silk-and-bamboo
plane. He successfully completed his
spectacular air stunt from Portland to
Vancouver Barracks in twelve minutes.

"Rooftop Spectacular"

On the twenty-fifth anniversary of Christofferson's rooftop flight, the Portland *Oregonian* editorialized that the flight (shown here) "will be long-remembered . . . as it has never been done again, and probably never will."

However, eighty-three years after the original stunt, the Pearson Field Historical Society organized a repeat of this remarkable event. On September 16, 1995, Tom Murphy flew a replica of the Curtiss pusher from the roof of the same Multnomah Hotel to Vancouver's Pearson Field.

Oregon Historical Society, neg.#62776

Oregon Historical Society, neg.#24281

Silas Christofferson, Rooftop Runway

Christofferson and his wife, Edna, moved to San Francisco after his famous Portland–Vancouver flight. There he opened a flying school and continued his aerial adventures. Christofferson was primarily an aeronautical engineer whose designs showed steady improvement. This "air pioneer" was killed in 1916 while testing a plane in the Bay Area.

Airmail Postcard, August 10, 1912

Pioneer aviator Walter Edwards carried 1,500 letters from Portland to Vancouver in an official U.S. mail sack hanging from the plane. Edwards made the same trip the following day with another 1,000 pieces of mail.

Jim Raley Collection

Model Airplane, c. 1912

This large-scale model is believed to have been used in designing the Curtiss pusher aircraft that Silas Christofferson flew from the roof of the Multnomah Hotel on June 11, 1912. Made of Goodyear aircraft fabric, this was a working model with movable controls.

U.S. Mail Service, August 10, 1912

Following the dawn of aviation, the carrying of mail by air became inevitable. Flights for such purposes were merely stunts until the first regular airmail routes between New York and Washington, D.C., began in 1918. Walter Edwards, shown in this photo, was the first to carry U.S. mail officially by air across state boundaries. He flew from Waverly Country Club in southeast Portland to Vancouver Barracks.

Jim Raley Collection

THOSE BARNSTORMING DAYS ⁓ The two decades between 1919 and 1939 are sometimes referred to as the "Golden Age of Flight." Men and women took to the air, establishing record-breaking flights for speed, distance, and altitude. Commercial aviation and airmail delivery also developed during this era.

Veterans from the skies of France helped pioneer the cause of aviation in the United States after World War I. These "barnstorming" aerial acrobats, who risked their lives in flying circuses across America, introduced aviation to the public.

Beginning in 1911, early experiments in powered flight took place at Vancouver Barracks, on the grassy field beside the Columbia River. When the spruce production plant, which occupied this site during World War I, was dismantled after the war, flying resumed at the field.

Commercial flying developed alongside the military field. Vancouver was an important stop on the nation's first airmail service route. The U.S. Army operated the Three-hundred Twenty-first Observation Squadron, a reserve unit, from Pearson Field until 1941.

"Tuning Up a U.S. Army Aeroplane," Postcard

Aircarft maintenance was an important part of reserve army fliers' routine at Pearson Field.

TUNING UP A U. S. ARMY AEROPLANE.   SERIES NO. 12   222671

Vancouver National Historic Reserve Trust

Plane Crash, Vancouver Barracks

Pioneer aviation was a risky profession, but one that afforded financial opportunity. Pilots were promptly hired to replace those who were killed—which happened quite frequently.

Vancouver National Historic Reserve Trust

Lt. Oakley G. Kelly

After the First World War, the army began to train reserves for Army Air Service, the air branch of the army formerly known as the Aviation Section of the Signal Corps. At Vancouver Barracks, future site of Pearson Field, the grassy expanse beside the Columbia River began its role as a military airstrip. The army established an air forest patrol at the barracks in 1921.

Oakley Kelly was in charge of aviation at the army post from 1924 to 1928. Kelly had completed the first nonstop flight across the continent the previous year—from New York to Los Angeles—in less than twenty-seven hours.

AERIAL AGE

VOL. 16, No. 1   January, 1923   25 CENTS A COPY

Aviation and The Feminine Touch

Maintenance and Operating Equipment of Airplane and Seaplane Stations

Flying Between Canada and the United States

England Builds Giant Torpedo Plane

AVIATION PAYS ITS WAY

A noteworthy article by Conway W. Cooke, showing clearly how other industries are benefitting through aeronautic research and development.

Aerial Age, **January 1923**

Hundreds of aviation magazines, such as *Aerial Age* (earlier known as *Aerial Age Weekly*), were published in the first decades of the twentieth century to feed the interest in this new mode of transportation.

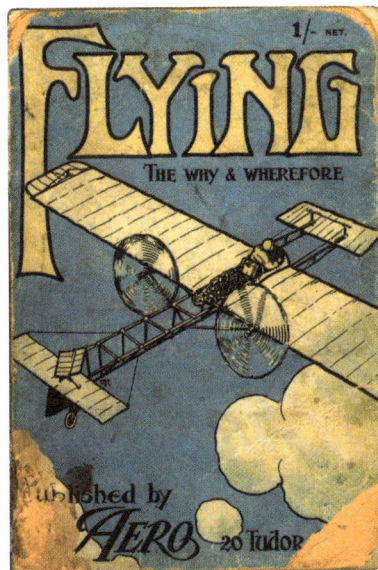

Sheet Music and Books

Flying captured the popular
imagination, with songs,
novels, and sheet music
devoted to the subject.

"Airplane Passenger Flights" Advertisement, Vancouver *Evening Columbian*, April 12, 1924

Flight was still new to most people in the
1920s, and aerial exhibitions drew large crowds.
Thousands of people came out to the flying
field at Vancouver Barracks on weekends.

Vancouver pioneer flyer Bill Moore
explained: "The main idea was to ferry
passengers." Barnstorming refers to "landing
in farmer's fields"—close enough to town to
draw people out and "get 'em to fly. . . .
We'd put on these air shows."

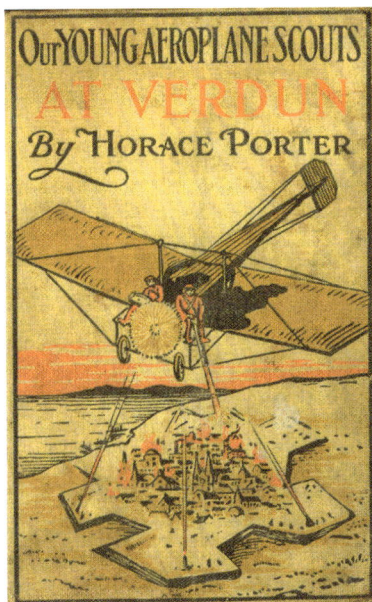

ARMY AIR SERVICE AT PEARSON FIELD

Former World War I fighter pilots helped shape the future of the Army Air Service at Vancouver Barracks. A large number of inexpensive airplanes surplused after World War I made flying accessible to many civilians, and interest in aviation among the American public increased. Flying schools became popular for men and women alike. The nation's fledgling airmail and passenger service developed during the next two decades.

Commercial aviation began alongside the army airfield after 1925. Vancouver served as a distribution point for Northwest airmail service.

Pacific Air Transport, Vancouver
by Dale Denny

Private companies began contracting with the federal government to deliver airmail across the United States following passage of the 1925 Contract Air Mail Act and the 1926 Air Commerce Act.

In 1925, the Vancouver Chamber of Commerce began operation of a flying field just east of the military field for commercial and mail uses, with the expectation that it would "place Vancouver on the air map of the Pacific Coast," according to the May 14, 1925, Vancouver *Evening Columbian.* Portland did not have an airfield at that time.

In September 1926, Pacific Air Transport began regular airmail service, making Vancouver a main stop on the nation's first "CAM" (contract airmail) routes.

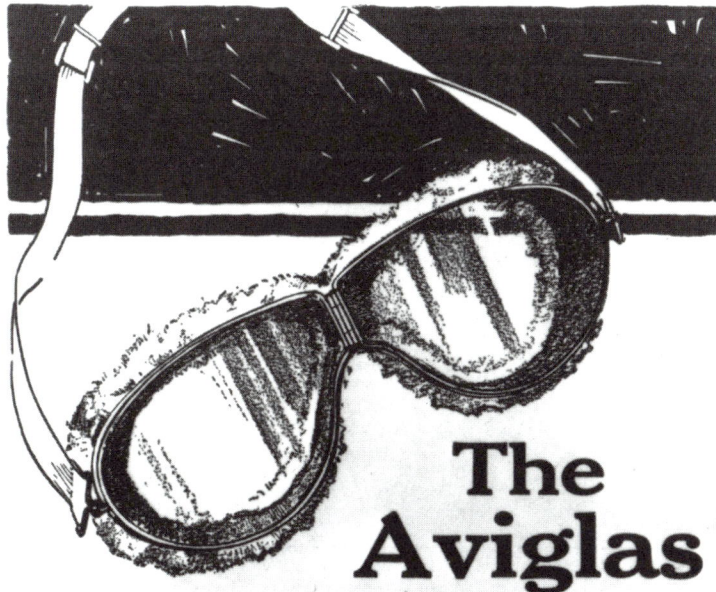

The Aviglas

Trade Mark Reg. U. S Pat. Off.
Patented Jan. 22nd, 1918

The Aviation Goggle ordered by the Government for the use of
the Flying Officers, Pilots and Observers
of the United States Army

THE MOST IMPORTANT THING FOR THE AVIATOR
IS TO BE ABLE TO SEE CLEARLY AND DISTINCTLY

Write to us for illustrations and prices on the various types.

Designed and patented by

F. A. HARDY & CO.

JOHN H. HARDIN, President

Dept. M.   P. O. Box 804   CHICAGO, ILL.

Oregon Historical Society, neg.#94311

"The Aviglas" Advertisement, *Aerial Age Weekly*, March 11, 1918

New products, such as the goggles shown here, were manufactured to meet the increased interest in flying.

A surplus of military aircraft existed when World War I ended. Thousands of Curtiss JN-4s—commonly called "Jennies"—flooded the market. They were offered for sale in magazines such as *Aerial Age Weekly*. Bill Moore recalled that "for five hundred dollars you could buy them. They would come in crates."

The January 29, 1918, Vancouver *Daily Columbian* remarked: "The tremendous strides in the building of aeroplanes . . . make possible almost any kind of prediction to their future use. . . . In the early days [of aviation], 35 to 40 miles an hour was fast. . . . Tomorrow it may be 200."

Oregon Historical Society

Early Airmail Flight Suit

This fur-lined, heavy cotton-twill flight suit kept pilots warm in the unheated cabins of early aircraft.

Pearson Field Dedication, September 16, 1925

Lt. Oakley Kelly promoted and staged elaborate community flying events. He had a special chance to put his showmanship to work for the Pearson Field dedication, which he predicted would draw "the second largest assemblage of airships in the country's history." Twenty-five thousand people were expected to view a "mammoth flying circus," according to the September 14, 1925, Vancouver *Evening Columbian.*

The field was named in honor of Lt. Alexander Pearson, a young aviator who had been killed in a flying accident the previous year. Pearson had attended high school in Vancouver, and his widow, parents, and brother were on hand for the dedication ceremonies. Schools closed for the all-day event.

Early Vancouver Airmail Envelopes and Postage Stamps

The world's first stamp designed for airmail was issued in 1918. Special surcharges were added for airmail delivery. The cost was twenty-four cents for the first ounce at a time when regular postage was a penny. The domestic airmail category ended in 1977.

Jim Raley Collection

AIR BRIDGE ACROSS THE ARCTIC ⌐ In the midst of army and civilian aviation activities at Pearson Field, a chance event riveted world attention on Vancouver. The historic moment came on a drizzly Sunday morning in June 1937. Three Russian fliers emerged from a strange-looking airplane that had just completed one of aviation's greatest achievements—the first nonstop flight over the North Pole.

The people-to-people diplomacy created by this landmark flight helped generate goodwill between the United States and the Soviet Union as world tensions grew prior to World War II.

Vancouver National Historic Reserve Trust, Dale Denny Collection

Transpolar Flight Landing Site, Pearson Field
by Dale Denny

The Russian fliers of 1937 headed toward Pearson Field when they found they would run out of fuel before reaching their planned San Francisco destination. Valeri Chkalov, pilot, preferred Vancouver's military airfield over Portland's Swan Island airport because it afforded greater security. Soldiers guarded the huge plane and kept the crowds away. Shortly after the plane arrived, autos were parked on every available side road in town, and the Interstate Bridge was jammed.

The fliers received attention from the world's leaders and press after their successful landing. Gen. George C. Marshall was head of Vancouver Barracks when this unexpected event occurred.

**Russian Transpolar Flight Landing,
Pearson Field, June 20, 1937**

by Dale Denny

Three Soviet aviators—pilot Valeri Chkalov, copilot Georgiy Baidukov, and navigator Alexander Belyakov—flew an ANT-25 monoplane nonstop from Moscow to Vancouver, Washington, in sixty-three hours and sixteen minutes. This dangerous mission marked a milestone in aviation history. It led to now-routine over-the-pole flights, which have changed the world's transportation patterns.

Tin and Biscuit, Russian Transpolar Flight, 1937

This tin was carried by the three Russian aviators on their epochal flight to America.

Scale Model of Vancouver's First Monument to the Transpolar Flight

by Dale Denny

During the winter of 1937, the Vancouver community organized a "Moscow to Vancouver" committee. Its purpose was to raise $15,000 to erect a monument at Pearson Field to commemorate the transpolar-flight landing of the Russian fliers. The scale model of the monument, prepared by Victor Schneider of Portland, was on display for several months. World War II intervened, however, and the monument was never built. This is the only known surviving photo of that unrealized community effort.

In 1975, Vancouver citizens succeeded in building another monument now located at Pearson Field. Many important commercial ties and cultural exchanges with our Russian neighbors across the North Pacific have resulted from this initiative.

CHAPTER FIVE
KAISER SHIPYARD

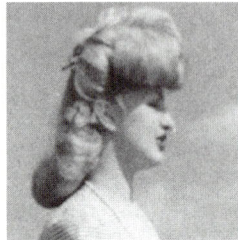  

World War II Transforms Vancouver

The entry of the United States into World War II necessitated a rapid buildup of the nation's naval forces. Attracted by inexpensive Northwest hydropower, the War Department chose Vancouver and Portland as locations for three huge shipyards. Fur and timber had accelerated economic growth in prior decades. Now another Northwest natural resource—abundant water from the Columbia—provided the raw power for much-needed electricity. The first federal dams on the Columbia supplied hydropower to war industries in the Northwest, among them shipbuilding, aluminum manufacture, and plutonium production at Hanford.

Vancouver Kaiser Shipyard

The Kaiser Company had a proven track record with government contracts and was selected by the U.S. Maritime Commission to build ships.

In January 1942, shipyard construction began on the site of a former dairy farm east of Vancouver Barracks, transforming the area into a "giant tool" of the war effort. The shipyard was located just upstream from earlier shipbuilding activities of the Hudson's Bay Company and the World War I eras. Incredibly, the yard was completed— at a cost of $17 million—and the first ship launched in just 165 days. Kaiser built ships faster and at lower cost than other companies. Within a year, the yard expanded from eight shipways to twelve.

Vancouver was the second of three Kaiser shipyards built in the Portland/Vancouver area. Oregon Shipbuilding Corporation (a Henry Kaiser partnership) opened a shipyard in St. John's in 1941. Kaiser Company, Inc. (KCI) operated the yards in Vancouver and at Swan Island in Portland. Swan Island followed Vancouver in opening production in March 1942.

Engineering Office, Kaiser Company, Vancouver

Many occupations with technical and engineering expertise were required to build ships. By the war's end, Vancouver Kaiser had launched 141 vessels of five types: cargo Liberty Ships, LSTs (Landing Ship Tank), Escort Aircraft Carriers (Baby Flat Tops), Attack Transports, and Troop Transports.

Clark County Museum

Arrival at Work, Vancouver Shipyard

by Louis Lee

Kaiser operated around-the-clock, three shifts a day, seven days a week. Employment peaked at nearly 39,000 workers in December 1943. Kaiser recruited nationwide, and special trains brought workers to Vancouver and Portland.

Shipyard workers Leona Ellis and Patricia Koehler recalled: "That place was so big . . . it was just another world; here there were thousands of people coming through these gates."

Vancouver National Historic Reserve Trust, Louis Lee Collection

Vancouver National Historic Reserve Trust

The Ships We Build Booklet

This publication describes the types of ships built at the Vancouver Kaiser yard and gives a chronological listing of ships produced through 1944.

Henry J. Kaiser and Eleanor Roosevelt, Vancouver
by Louis Lee

Mrs. Roosevelt came to Vancouver to christen the
Alazon Bay on April 5, 1943. The ship, later renamed
USS *Casablanca*, was the first of the Baby Flat Tops,
or small aircraft carriers. The Vancouver yard became
known for its production of these vessels, which
played a major role in the European and South
Pacific conflicts. Pres. Franklin D. Roosevelt also
visited Portland and Vancouver during the war years.

KAISER COMPANY, INC. (KCI) ⬩ Henry J. Kaiser
(1882–1967), originally from upstate New York,
was an industrialist with little formal education.
He got his start by running photography studios
for the tourist trade. Later, he moved to Spokane,
Washington, and entered the hardware business.
Kaiser's operations grew in the early part of the
twentieth century from road construction, dams,
cement, steel, and aluminum plants to
shipbuilding. Kaiser was a successful government
contractor who also tried to meet his workers'
needs for housing, child care, transportation, and
medical care. Kaiser received national recognition
with his flare for publicity and the speed with
which his company built ships.

Woman Riveters and Drillers, April 8, 1945

The Kaiser Company promoted safety in the workplace through posters and in the company newsletter, the *Bo's'n's Whistle*. First-aid stations were set up in the yards, and workers wore protective goggles, special helmets, leather aprons, and gloves, depending on the task. Note the bandannas in this photo. Women tied their hair up to keep it out of their eyes, and out of the machinery.

The shipyard was a noisy place. There was a constant din from activity taking place twenty-four hours a day.

Welding, Ship Construction

Kaiser provided training for its workers, whether welding, pipe fitting, or plumbing. Joining ship plates by welding was close-quarters work.

Lue Rayne Culbertson, Kaiser employee, recalled her work from the World War II era: "Really, welding is a beautiful art. . . . It was a real, real satisfying job."

WE ARE THE HOME-FRONT ARMY, 1942–1945

With men fighting overseas, women responded to the national emergency and entered the workforce in unprecedented numbers. The Portland and Vancouver yards recruited women earlier and in greater numbers than any other shipbuilding center in the United States.

By 1944, 20,000 women were on the job, a fifth of the workforce at the three area shipyards. Both government and industry wooed women to war work. The media portrayed women as strong and capable, with campaigns such as "Rosie the Riveter" and "We Can Do It!" Women and men were paid equally for equal work.

Oregon Historical Society, neg.#6130

Maritime Commission, Ships-for-Victory Pins, Award Pin, and War-Bond Button

The workforce from the Portland and Vancouver shipyards received many awards for distinguished service from the U.S. Maritime Commission. In addition, workers participated in war-bond and Red Cross drives to support the war effort.

Shift Change at the "Short-Order" Shipyard (opposite)

Good morale in the yards, and competition between them, contributed to their record-smashing achievements. From keel laying to launching, the Vancouver shipyard once built an LST in seventy-one-and-a-half hours!

Henry Kaiser spoke of his employees: "With hands and hearts they are fashioning complete victory as surely as if they were on the fighting front."

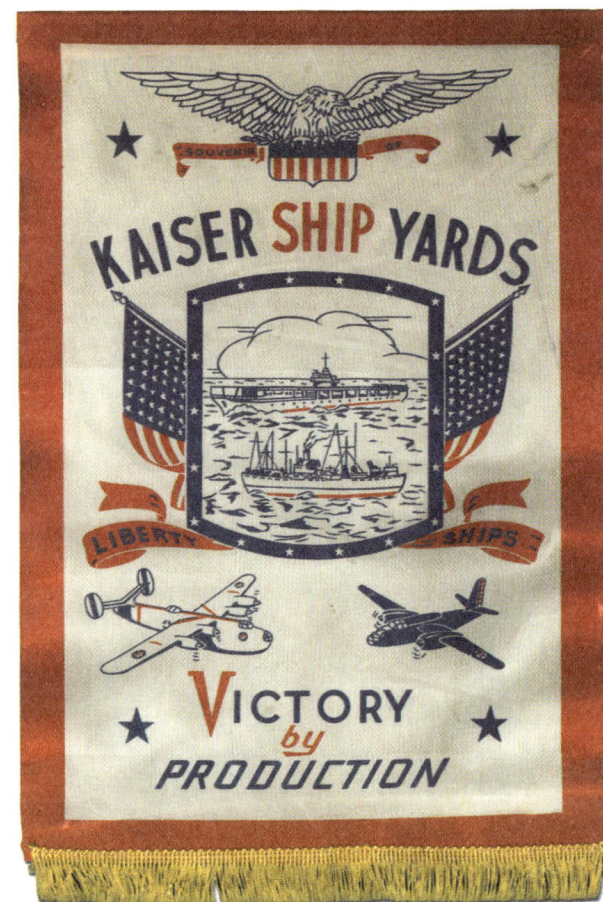

Kaiser Shipyard Souvenir Wall Hanging

Souvenir items supporting the war effort were popular with workers on the home front.

Army Retail Store Advertisement, *Columbian*, July 15, 1942

The need for stores and services increased dramatically in Vancouver as workers arrived for shipyard employment. A new shopping center in McLoughlin Heights received national recognition for its innovative design.

Aluminum Hat, Kaiser Shipyard

Workplace safety was important to Kaiser. Workers wore mandatory masks, goggles, hats, protective clothing, and face shields for certain jobs.

A columnist in the *Oregon Journal* remarked, "Those tin hats . . . cost on average three dollars apiece."

Identification Badge, Vancouver Kaiser Shipyard

Badges were color-coded to indicate the worker's shift. Swing-shift wages were 10 percent higher and night-shift 15 percent higher than day-shift pay.

How'dy Stranger Booklet, Kaiser Company, Vancouver

Kaiser gave each new employee a copy of this little book, full of useful information on such topics as wage scales, shift schedules, insurance, war bonds, housing, transportation, schools, hospitals, and descriptions of principal crafts and trades at the yard.

Cardboard Lunch Pail Used at Vancouver Kaiser Shipyard

Workers carried their own meals to eat during their shift. The *Bo's'n's Whistle* devoted space to advocating good nutrition and to food recommendations: "Good food—the right food—can help put more 'power' into America's manpower!"

Oregon Historical Society, neg.#78702

Child Service Center, Parent-Teacher Conference

Kaiser shipyards provided carefully designed and well-equipped child-care centers to attract and hold its female workers. The centers operated around-the-clock, seven days a week. They served children from ages eighteen months to six years, as well as school-age children ages six to twelve before and after school, on holidays, and during summers. The child-care program was supported by the Kaiser Company and the U.S. Maritime Commission. Workers paid $5 per week for one child and $3.75 for each additional child.

In operation for just two years, from November 1943 until September 1945, the child service centers received national attention and recognition. This model program was professionally staffed with early childhood education teachers, dietitians, and registered nurses recruited from across the United States.

A child's day was balanced between activity, meals, and rest. A midmorning "bracer" of fruit juice and cod-liver oil was designed to build "strong healthy children." The centers even offered a "Home Service Food" program, which sold parents precooked meals at cost (fifty cents per portion). This idea proved very popular for tired mothers returning home from the shipyard at shift's end. The meal for Wednesday, March 15, 1944, was fresh salmon loaf with lemon and avocado gelatin salad.

World War II Ration Stamp Books and Tokens

Meat, dairy products, sugar, canned goods, gasoline, and other items were rationed during the war. Households registered for their stamp books, and each family member was issued both a book and blue and red tokens. Vancouver resident Frances Harris remembered: "We had to figure points along with the money. Scarce things took more points." The average citizen was allowed around ten gallons of gas per month. Posters urged households to save kitchen grease (for use in manufacturing bombs) and reminded everyone that "rubber is precious, treat it accordingly."

Clark County Museum

VANCOUVER'S POPULATION EXPLODES ≈

Vancouver's population grew from 18,000 to more than 90,000 during World War II, as workers arrived—often bringing just a suitcase—from all parts of the nation to help win the war on the home front. Housing, schools, churches, stores, and other services expanded to accommodate shipyard employees. The war years completely changed the character of Vancouver from a small, sleepy town to a larger, diverse community. It was a boom period.

Clark County Museum

McLoughlin Heights, Looking North from MacArthur and Andresen Streets

The city council created the Vancouver Housing Authority (VHA) in 1942 to administer the construction of massive temporary and permanent housing projects. McLoughlin Heights was the second largest wartime housing project in the nation. Homes rented for $36 to $45 per month. The VHA allowed racially integrated housing. Kaiser provided bus transportation for workers to the shipyard. The housing projects' "look-alike houses on look-alike streets" confused people's sense of direction, and more than one resident came home to the wrong house!

Under the guidance of local attorney and civic leader D. Elwood Caples, the VHA provided a national model known as the "Vancouver Plan" for postwar housing administered by the federal Public Housing Administration. The VHA still exists today.

Vancouver School Classroom during World War II

When the Kaiser shipyard came to Vancouver, the local school system was forced to adjust quickly. Vancouver's World War II–era school district was one of the nation's most profoundly affected. The U.S. Office of Education supplied emergency funds. The district went from 200 to 1,000 teachers. Before the war was over, nearly every school in the system was double-shifted.

Vancouver teacher Helen Holcomb recalled: "These were extraordinary times." In buildings designed for 500 students, "they tried to teach 800. . . . Two drinking fountains for 500 to 600 youngsters." By the end of the war, Vancouver's citizens had widened their horizons through contacts with people from other parts of the nation. One Vancouver classroom included forty pupils representing twenty-six states!

Clark County Museum

Clark County Museum

Boy Playing Horseshoes, Vancouver Housing Authority

Recreation centers kept school-aged children occupied while their parents worked. Activities such as talent shows, dance classes, music lessons, and sports ran day and night in various war-housing community centers. VHA personnel organized "Victory Gardens" and home beautification projects.

AT THE SHIPYARD ～ The Kaiser Company was able to build ships with such speed because it ignored traditional production methods and used an assembly-line approach. Ships were built in separate sections and welded together in a few days. Kaiser took care of workers' medical needs by building a hospital adjacent to the yard and offering a prepaid health plan for employees and their families. Monthly rates were $3.50. After the war, the medical plan was offered to the public, and Kaiser Permanente became a national leader in prepaid medical care. At age eighty-five, Henry Kaiser looked back on his many achievements and remarked: "Of all the things I've done, I expect only to be remembered for my hospitals."

Vancouver Shipyard Workers at the USS *Alazon Bay* Launching, April 5, 1943 (opposite)

A crowd estimated at between 65,000 and 75,000 people turned out to see first lady Eleanor Roosevelt christen the ship *Alazon Bay*, the first of the Baby Flat Tops to slide down the ways at Vancouver.

Clark County Museum

Ship Launch down the Ways
by Louis Lee

Most jobs at the shipyard were covered by a master contract between the Kaiser Company, the U.S. Maritime Commission, and the American Federation of Labor. Union-scale pay rates averaged $1.08 to $1.33 per hour. These were good wages at a time when most jobs paid on a average of only $0.76 per hour.

The first ship launched at the Vancouver yard was christened the SS *George Vancouver* on July 4, 1942. The last ship slid into the water on November 24, 1946.

Vancouver National Historic Reserve Trust, Louis Lee Collection

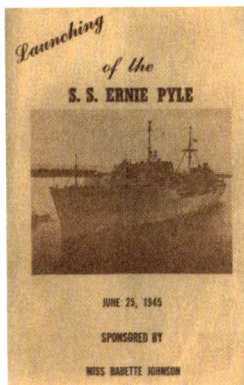

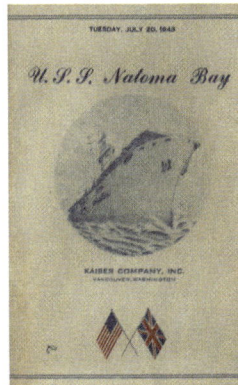

Vancouver National Historic Reserve Trust

Ship Launch Programs

The Kaiser Company produced special printed programs for ship launches. Each launch ceremony included a sponsor, a maid or matron of honor, and attendants to present flowers.

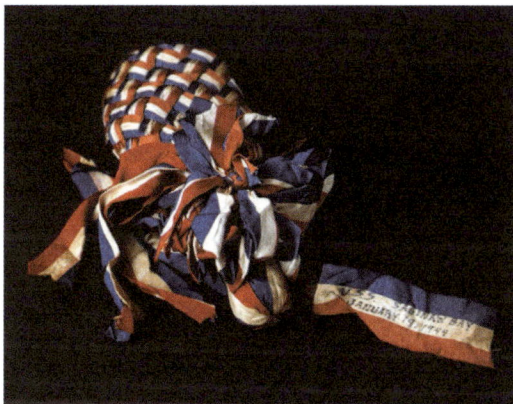

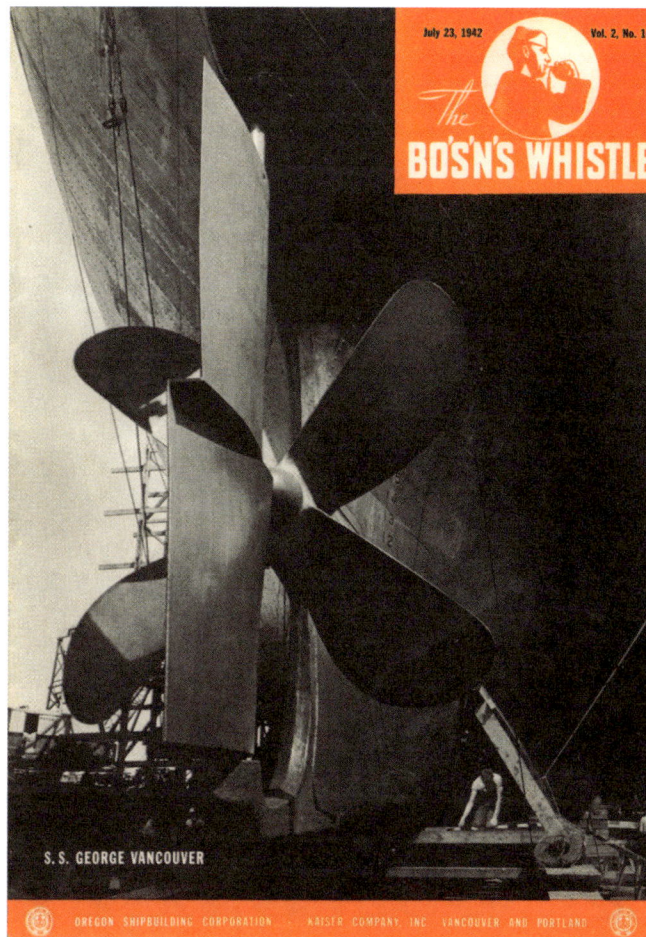

S.S. GEORGE VANCOUVER

OREGON SHIPBUILDING CORPORATION · KAISER COMPANY, INC · VANCOUVER AND PORTLAND

Kaiser Company Photographer, Louis Lee

Henry Kaiser had a penchant for publicity and knew how to use his public-relations skills. The company newsletter, the *Bo's'n's Whistle*, pamphlets, and posters were important communication tools. A regular column, "At Kaiser Yard," appeared in the Vancouver *Columbian* newspaper.

Louis Lee, chief photographer for the Kaiser shipyard, covered the launching of every ship built at Vancouver.

Ribbon-wrapped Champagne Bottle, Vancouver Kaiser Shipyard

This bottle was used to christen the Baby Flat Top USS *Saginaw Bay* on January 19, 1944. The proper launching of a ship was very important, for "it is a well known old nautical superstition that bad luck attends the vessel not properly christened," the *Bo's'n's Whistle* advised in May 1942.

Portland's *Oregon Journal* explained in May 1943: "Sometimes the bottle did not break and Edgar Kaiser would grab it and hurl it at the fast-moving ship as it slipped down the ways."

The *Bo's'n's Whistle*, Kaiser Company Employee Newsletter

The *Bo's'n's Whistle* was launched on July 18, 1941. It served as an important communication tool and morale booster for all three Portland and Vancouver shipyards. The newsletter was published biweekly and, later, weekly throughout the war.

**Woman Shipyard Workers,
May 28, 1944**

Kaiser surveyed its female workers to learn
how they felt about losing their industrial
jobs at war's end. Most said "they intend
to make a full time job of keeping house,"
the *Bo's'n's Whistle* reported.

**The *Pulse*, October 1, 1943, Northern Permanente
Foundation Newsletter**

In 1933, Henry Kaiser began providing medical care for
his employees working on Hoover Dam. One of the
Kaiser Company's first hospitals was in Vancouver, built
for the shipyard workers and their families.

Kaiser Permanente survived and prospered as a
nonprofit health-care organization after World War II.
It became a national model for the health maintenance
organizations that have changed the shape of medical
care in the United States.

"Permanente" comes from the name of a creek in
Santa Clara County, California, which the Kaiser
Company used for its cement-plant operations.

⟡ During the war years, Vancouver Barracks served as a point of embarkation for soldiers going overseas. The military built Barnes General Hospital, located in the northern part of the reservation, during this time. After the Three-hundred Twenty-first Reserve Observation Unit was called to active service in 1941, Pearson Field was no longer used as an operational airfield or air-reserve training facility. The Kaiser shipyards provide one of the most dramatic labor stories of our nation's history.

Clark County Museum

Musical Performance, Vancouver Housing Authority

Top bands visited Vancouver to provide dance music for entertainment-hungry crowds.

"Welcome to Vancouver Barracks Armed Forces Lounge" Sign

This sign was preserved from the Officers Club lounge during renovation of the O.O. Howard House in the 1990s.

Officers Club, Vancouver Barracks

The *Challenger*, Vancouver Barracks' newsletter during World War II, described the grand reopening of the Officers Club as "an extremely gala [occasion]. . . . The dinner was . . . epicurean in selection and preparation."

The Officers Club is now known as the Gen. O.O. Howard House.

Clark County Museum, Carlton Bond Collection

USO Girls on a B-17 Wing

This photo, taken in Hawaii during World War II, belonged to Capt. Carlton Bond, who commanded Pearson Field from 1929 to 1933 and from 1938 to 1940.

The USO (United Service Organizations) is a civilian, congressionally chartered nonprofit organization. It was founded in 1941 to provide assistance to men and women in the U.S. armed forces and their families. During World War II, the USO operated in Vancouver at Seventh and Reserve streets.

CHAPTER SIX
A SENSE OF PLACE

Officers Row Renovation, 1988

Local citizens helped save Officers
Row for the city of Vancouver in the
1980s, and in the 1990s efforts began
to preserve the entire breadth of
public land that now makes up the
reserve. Officers Row is a nationally
recognized model for adaptive reuse
of historic public properties.

LOCAL EFFORTS PRESERVE SITE ⌒ Determined and
persistent preservation efforts in the twentieth century have
led to the present Vancouver National Historic Reserve.

Attempts were already under way at the turn of the
century to recognize Fort Vancouver and the fur-trade and
settlement era it represented. In 1910, local citizens placed a
commemorative stone monument near the fort site. The
exact location of the fort was unknown then. Periodic
initiatives by local groups, including the Fort Vancouver
Historical Society, the Oregon Historical Society, and the
Washington State Historical Society, continued through the
1920s and 1930s in an effort to acknowledge the national
importance of Fort Vancouver. Congress designated the site
as Fort Vancouver National Monument, a unit of the
National Park Service, in 1948. Thirteen years later, it was
redesignated a national historic site. In the fall of 1996,
Congress established the Vancouver National Historic
Reserve.

Site of "Old Fort Vancouver," April 30, 1908

George Himes, of the Oregon Historical Society (on right), examines the general location of the former Hudson's Bay Company headquarters in the Oregon Country.

Oregon Historical Society, neg.#94312

Dedication of Reconstructed Fort Vancouver Bastion, April 1974

Rep. Julia Butler Hansen was instrumental in obtaining federal appropriations to reconstruct Fort Vancouver.

Oregon Historical Society, neg.#94313

158

1925 Centennial Celebration, Vancouver

Efforts by the local chamber of commerce and civic leaders to stage a summer celebration commemorating the one-hundredth anniversary of Fort Vancouver's founding began in the spring of 1925. Festivities included this parade and a community dinner. A special centennial coin was struck at the U.S. Mint in San Francisco.

1925 Fort Vancouver Centennial Coin

Jack Urquhart of Vancouver prepared the drawings for the souvenir fifty-cent piece commemorating Fort Vancouver's centennial. Pearson Field commander, Lt. Oakley Kelly, delivered the coins on a record-breaking flight to San Francisco (round trip in ten hours and fifty-five minutes).

Centennial organizers sold approximately 15,000 coins for a dollar each to help finance local activities.

Clark County Museum

ON THE HISTORIC RESERVE

TODAY ~ Historic places and cultural landscapes— such as the reserve— are powerful and tangible reminders of the past. An annual calendar of community events brings strength and vitality to this place, engaging visitors and students alike.

Vancouver Barracks Parade Grounds and Reconstructed Bandstand

The Vancouver community takes pride in the well-maintained buildings and parklike setting of the historic reserve.

Vancouver Barracks Parade Grounds

Military reenactments bring to life the daily activities of the nineteenth-century U.S. Army

160

Fort Vancouver National Historic Site

Fort Vancouver Excavation Site and Palisade

Reconstruction of the fort began in 1966 with the north palisade. All reconstructions were based on extensive archaeological investigations and historical documentation. In 1948, when Congress established the national monument, the main focus was to preserve the Hudson's Bay Company site and the archaeological resources underground. At that time, there was no precedent for reconstruction of lost historic structures by the federal government. However, community interest and the work of Rep. Julia Butler Hansen shifted the focus of the National Park Service at Fort Vancouver toward reconstruction. An active building program took place in the 1970s with budgets secured on Representative Hansen's initiative.

Fort Vancouver National Historic Site

Fort Vancouver National Historic Site

Brigade Encampment

This special event began in the summer of 1980 and re-creates the life of nineteenth-century Hudson's Bay Company fur trappers and traders.

Living-history demonstrations by interpreters dressed in period clothing were a natural outgrowth of the 1970s' reconstruction activity. Interpreters re-create life at Fort Vancouver in 1845, providing a new historical ambience for visitors. The fort's legendary candlelight tour started in 1983 and continues to grow in popularity each year, allowing visitors to savor the past while enjoying the present.

Fur-Store Interior, Fort Vancouver National Historic Site

The fur-store reconstruction was completed in 1994 and provides an opportunity for visitors to understand the fur trade in a re-created historical setting. The building also houses Fort Vancouver's curatorial division and archaeological collection, which contains more than a million artifacts, the largest collection of recovered Hudson's Bay Company material in the world.

City of Vancouver, Water Resources Center Programs

Present-day students learn about one of the earth's most precious resources—water—along the shore of the Columbia River.

Loren Nelson

Pearson Air Museum at the Jack Murdock Aviation Center

A 23,500-square-foot museum and educational facility opened in 1997, in rebuilt and historic hangars, to commemorate the story of flight at the historic reserve.

Larry Rank

Larry Rank

U.S. Army

Larry Rank

Vancouver Barracks, 2001

Vancouver Barracks buildings no longer needed by the military will be turned over to the city of Vancouver. The reserve partners and trust, together with the community, are committed to preserving and interpreting the historic site while adapting the properties for new uses.

(top) Double Artillery Barracks, 1907
(middle) Infantry Barracks, 1887
(bottom) American Red Cross Convalescent House, 1918

BIBLIOGRAPHY

This bibliography lists most sources consulted in the four-year-long exhibit project.

Much of the research labor associated with exhibition development is typically "lost" after exhibits are constructed and opened. With this bibliography, we make an effort to document and "preserve" most of the sources used in staging "One Place across Time." The bibliography is arranged according to the following categories:

    I. Books, pamphlets

    II. Articles, newspapers, periodicals

    III. Unpublished theses, papers, musical scores, manuscripts

    IV. Public documents

    V. Sound and video recordings, Internet sources

I. BOOKS, PAMPHLETS

Alderson, William T., ed. *Mermaids, Mummies and Mastodons: The Emergence of the American Museum*. Washington, D.C.: American Association of Museums, 1992.

Alexander, Edward Porter. *Museum Masters: Their Museums and Their Influence*. Nashville, Tenn.: American Association for State and Local History, 1983.

Alinda, James, ed. *Carleton E. Watkins: Photographs of the Columbia River and Oregon*. Carmel, Calif.: Friends of Photography in association with the Weston Gallery, 1979.

Allen, John Logan. *Passage through the Garden: Lewis and Clark and the Image of the American Northwest*. Urbana: University of Illinois Press, 1975.

American Association of Museums Technical Information Service. *The Audience in Exhibition Development: Course Proceedings from Training Program Developed by the Office of Museum Programs, Smithsonian Institution*. Washington, D.C., American Association of Museums, 1992.

Ames, Kenneth L., Barbara Franco, and Thomas Frye, eds. *Ideas and Images: Developing Interpretive History Exhibits*. Washington, D.C.: American Association of Museums, 1992.

Anderson, Marc. *Vancouver: A Pictorial History*. Norfolk, Va.: Dunning Co., 1983.

Anderson, Thomas McArthur. *Military and Civil Record of Thomas M. Anderson*. Vancouver, Wash.: Columbia Print, 1894. Copy at Vancouver National Historic Reserve Trust.

———. *Should Republics Have Colonies? An Address before the Oregon Commandery of the Loyal Legion, November 14, 1906*. Boston: A. T. Bliss & Co., 1906. Copy at Vancouver National Historic Reserve Trust.

Archdiocese Catholic Church in Oregon. *The Centenary: 100 Years of the Catholic Church in the Oregon Country*. Portland: Archdiocese Catholic Church in Oregon, 1939. Copy at Vancouver National Historic Reserve Trust.

Baidukov, Georgiy. *Russian Lindbergh: The Life of Valery Chkalov*. Smithsonian History of Aviation Series. Washington, D.C.: Smithsonian Institution Press, 1991.

Bailey, Ronald H., ed. *The Home Front: U.S.A.* Alexandria, Va.: Time-Life Books, 1977.

Bates, Nancy, comp. *Biography of Rev. George Henry Atkinson, D.D.: Journal of a Sea Voyage to Oregon in 1848 and Selected Addresses and Printed Articles*. Portland, Ore.: F. W. Baltes and Company, 1893.

Beals, Herbert K., trans. *Juan Perez on the Northwest Coast: Six Documents of His Expedition in 1774*. Portland: Oregon Historical Society Press, 1990.

Beecher, Henry W., and Anthony S. Wanrukiewicz. *U.S. Domestic Postal Rates, 1872–1992*. Shawnee-Mission, Kans.: Traditions Press, 1992.

Behrman, Carol H. *The Remarkable Writing Machine*. New York: Julian Messner, 1981.

Belcher, Edward. *Narrative of a Voyage Round the World, Performed in Her Majesty's Ship* Sulphur, *during the Years 1836–1842*. 2 vols. London: Henry Colburn, 1843.

Berliner, Don. *Distance Flights*. Minneapolis: Lerner Publications, 1990.

Binns, Archie. *Peter Skene Ogden: Fur Trader*. Portland, Ore.: Binfords and Mort, 1967.

Bland, Larry I., ed. *George Marshall: Interviews and Reminiscences for Forrest C. Pogue*. Lexington, Va.: George C. Marshall Research Foundation, 1991.

Bogdonoff, Nancy D. *Handwoven Textiles of Early New England*. Harrisburg, Pa.: Stackpole Books, 1975.

Bohrer, Walt. *Black Cats and Outside Loops: Tex Rankin, Aerobatic Ace*. Oregon City, Ore.: Plere Publishers, 1989.

Brooks–Pazmany, Kathleen. *United States Women in Aviation, 1919–1929*. Washington, D.C.: Smithsonian Institution Press, 1983.

Brown, Mark H. *The Flight of the Nez Perce*. Lincoln: University of Nebraska Press, 1967.

Buan, Carolyn, and Richard Lewis, eds. *The First Oregonians*. Portland: Oregon Council for the Humanities, 1991.

Bullock, Helen Duprey, ed. *The First Ladies Cookbook Favorite Recipes*. New York: Parents Magazine Press, 1969.

Bushnell, David I., Jr. *Drawings by George Gibbs in the Far Northwest, 1849–1851*. Miscellaneous Collections, no. 8. Washington, D.C.: Smithsonian Institution, 1938.

Carey, Charles H. *A General History of Oregon Prior to 1861*. 2 vols. Portland, Ore: Metropolitan Press, 1935–1936.

———, ed. *The Journals of Theodore Talbot, 1843 and 1849–52*. Portland, Ore: Metropolitan Press, 1931.

Carpenter, John A. *Sword and Olive Branch: Oliver Otis Howard*. Pittsburgh: University of Pittsburgh Press, 1999.

Chance, David, and Jennifer Chance. *Kanaka Village: Vancouver Barracks, 1974*. Office of Public Archaeology. Seattle: University of Washington, 1976.

Child Service Centers. Portland, Ore.: Kaiser Company, Inc., 1943. Copy at Vancouver National Historic Reserve Trust.

Choris, Louis. *Voyage Pittoresque Autour du Monde, Avec des Portraits de Sauvages . . . et Plusiers Objects d'Histoire Naturelle*. Paris: Didot, 1822.

Citizens Military Training Camps. *Memoirs of the CMTM*. 1935. Copy at Vancouver National Historic Reserve Trust.

Citizens Military Training Camps. *The Vanguard: First Annual Official Yearbook*. Vancouver Barracks, Wash., 1926.

Clark County Genealogical Society. *Clark County Census 1850 and 1860*. Vol. 1. U.S. Census of Oregon Territory, 1850, Washington Territory, 1860. Vancouver, Wash.: Clark County Genealogical Society, 1963.

Clark, Malcolm C., Jr., ed. and intro. *Pharisee among Philistines: The Diary of Judge Matthew P. Deady, 1871–1892*. Portland: Oregon Historical Society Press, 1975.

Clark, Robert. *River of the West: Stories from the Columbia*. New York: Harper Collins West, 1995.

Clarke County, Washington: Lewis and Clark Fair Edition. Vancouver, Wash.: J. H. Elwell, 1905. Copy at Vancouver National Historic Reserve Trust.

Clarke, S.A. *Pioneer Days of Oregon History*. Portland, Ore.: J. K. Gill Company, 1905.

Cline, Gloria Griffin. *Peter Skene Ogden and the Hudson's Bay Company*. Norman: University of Oklahoma Press, 1974.

Cohen, Stan. *The Tree Army: A Pictorial History of the CCC, 1933–1942*. Missoula, Mont.: Pictorial Histories Publishing Co., 1980.

Colman, Penny. *Rosie the Riveter: Women Working on the Home Front in World War II*. New York: Crown Publishers, 1995.

Cook, Warren. *Flood Tide of Empire: Spain and the Pacific Northwest, 1543–1819*. New Haven, Conn.: Yale University Press, 1973.

Corning, Howard McKinley, ed. *Dictionary of Oregon History*. Portland, Ore.: Binfords and Mort, 1956.

Coues, Elliot, ed. *The History of the Lewis and Clark Expedition: Meriwether Lewis and William Clark*. 1893. Reprint. New York: Dover Publications, 1965.

Cox, Ross. *The Columbia River . . . across the Continent*. Ed. by Edgar I. and Jane R. Stewart. 1882 text. Norman: University of Oklahoma Press, 1957.

Cray, Ed. *General of the Army: George C. Marshall, Soldier and Statesman*. New York: W. W. Norton and Company, 1990.

Cutright, Paul Russel. *A History of the Lewis and Clark Journals*. Norman: University of Oklahoma Press, 1976.

———. *Lewis and Clark, Pioneering Naturalists*. Lincoln: University of Nebraska Press, 1969.

Deady, Matthew P., ed. *General Laws of Oregon, 1845–1864*. Portland: Henry L. Pittock, State Printer, 1866.

Dedication Program, 1937 Soviet Transpolar Flight Monument. 20 June 1975. Vancouver, Wash. Copy at Vancouver National Historic Reserve Trust.

Delgado, James P. *The Beaver: First Steamship on the West Coast*. Victoria, British Columbia: Horsdal and Schubart, 1993.

Dietrich, William. *The Northwest Passage: The Great Columbia River*. New York: Simon and Schuster, 1995.

Douglas, David. *Journal Kept by David Douglas during His Travels in North America, 1823–1827*. London: William Wesley and Son, 1914.

Duncan, Janice K. *Minority without a Champion: Kanakas on the Pacific Coast, 1788–1850*. Portland: Oregon Historical Society Press, 1972.

Dunn, John. *The Oregon Territory and the British North American Fur Trade, with an Account of the Habits and Customs of the Principal Native Tribes on the Northern Continent*. Philadelphia: G. B. Zieber & Co., 1845.

Emerson, William K. *Encyclopedia of United States Army Insignia and Uniforms*. Norman: University of Oklahoma Press, 1996.

Erigero, Patricia. *Cultural Landscape Report: Fort Vancouver National Historic Site*. Vol. 2. Seattle: National Park Service, Department of the Interior, 1992.

Ermatinger, Edward. *Edward Ermatinger's York Factory Express Journal: Being a Record of Journeys Made between Fort Vancouver and the Hudson's Bay in the Years 1827–1828*. Transactions of the Royal Society of Canada. Vol. 6. Ottawa: Royal Society of Canada, 1912.

Evans, Steven Ross. *Voice of the Old Wolf: Lucullus Virgil McWhorter and the Nez Perce Indians*. Pullman: Washington State University Press, 1996.

The 50th Anniversary of the First USSR–USA Flight over the North Pole. Moscow: Novosti Press Agency Publishing House, 1987.

FitzGerald, Emily McCorkle. *An Army Doctor's Wife on the Frontier*. Ed. by Abe Laufe. Pittsburgh: University of Pittsburgh Press, 1962.

Fogdall, Alberta Brooks. *Royal Family of the Columbia: Dr. John McLoughlin and His Family*. Portland, Ore.: Binfords and Mort, 1978.

Foster, Mark S. *Henry J. Kaiser: Builder in the Modern American West*. American Studies Series. Austin: University of Texas Press, 1989.

Franchère, Gabriel. *Adventures at Astoria, 1810–1814*. Ed. and trans. by Hoyt C. Franchère. 1854 text. Norman: University of Oklahoma Press, 1967.

Gann, Ernest K. *The Aviator*. New York: Arbor House, 1981.

Gavin, Lettie. *American Women in World War I: They Also Served*. Niwot: University Press of Colorado, 1997.

George C. Marshall Lecture Series, 1988–1992. Vol. 1. Vancouver, Wash.: City of Vancouver, 1992.

George, Gerald. *Visiting History: Arguments over Museums and Historic Sites.* Washington, D.C.: American Association of Museums, 1990.

Gibson, James R. *Farming the Frontier: The Agricultural Opening of the Oregon Country, 1786–1846.* Seattle: University of Washington Press, 1985.

———. *Otter Skins, Boston Ships and China Goods: The Maritime Fur Trade of the Northwest Coast, 1785–1841.* Seattle: University of Washington Press, 1992.

Gildemeister, Jerry. *Avian Dreamers.* Union, Ore.: Bear Wallow Publishing Company, 1991.

Gill, John. *Dictionary of the Chinook Jargon.* Portland, Ore.: J.K. Gill, 1909.

Gilliss, Julia S. *So Far From Home: An Army Bride on the Western Frontier, 1865–1869.* Ed. by Priscilla Knuth. Portland: Oregon Historical Society Press, 1993.

"Good Work, Sister!" Women Shipyard Workers of World War II: An Oral History. Portland, Ore.: Northwest Women's History Project, 1982.

Gough, Barry M. *The Royal Navy and the Northwest Coast of North America, 1810–1914.* Vancouver: University of British Columbia Press, 1971.

Grant, U. S. *Personal Memoirs of U.S. Grant.* 2 vols. New York: Charles L. Webster and Company, 1885, 1886.

Gray, William H. *History of Oregon, 1792–1849.* Portland, Ore.: Harris and Holman, 1870.

Gunston, Bill. *Tupolev Aircraft.* Annapolis, Md.: Naval Institute Press, 1995.

Harper, J. Russell, ed. *Paul Kane's Frontier.* Austin: University of Texas Press, 1971.

Henderson, Heather. *General George C. Marshall: Statesman to the World.* Vancouver, Wash.: City of Vancouver, 1986.

Hendricks, Rickey Lynn. *A Model for National Health Care: The History of Kaiser Permanente.* New Brunswick, N.J.: Rutgers University Press, 1993.

Henry, John Frazier. *Early Maritime Artists of the Pacific Northwest Coast, 1741–1841.* Seattle: University of Washington Press, 1984.

Hibbs, Charles, and Bryn Thomas. *Report of Investigations of Excavations at Kanaka Village: Vancouver Barracks, Washington, 1980/1981.* Vol. 1. Olympia: Washington State Department of Transportation, 1984.

Hill, Beth. *The Remarkable World of Frances Barkley: 1769–1845.* Sidney, British Columbia: Gray's Publishing, 1978.

Hill, Edwin G. *In the Shadow of the Mountain: The Spirit of the CCC.* Pullman: Washington State University Press, 1990.

Holman, Frederick Van Voorhies. *Dr. John McLoughlin: The Father of Oregon.* Cleveland: Arthur H. Clark, 1907.

Housing in War and Peace: The Story of Public Housing in Vancouver, Washington. Vancouver, Wash.: City of Vancouver Housing Authority, 1972. Copy at Vancouver National Historic Reserve Trust.

Howard, O. O. *Autobiography of Oliver Otis Howard, Major General, United States Army.* New York: Baker & Taylor Company, 1908.

———. *My Life and Experiences among Our Hostile Indians: A Record of Personal Observations, Adventures, and Campaigns among the Indians of the Great West . . . and Customs in Peace and War.* Hartford, Conn.: A. D. Worthington and Company, 1907.

———. *Nez Perce Joseph . . . His Pursuit and Capture.* Boston: Lee and Shepard Publishers, 1881.

Howay, Frederic W., ed. *Voyages of the* Columbia *to the Northwest Coast, 1787–1790 and 1790–1793.* 1941. Reprint. Portland: Oregon Historical Society Press, 1990.

Hunn, Eugene S. *Nch'i-Wana: The Big River.* Seattle: University of Washington Press, 1990.

Hussey, John A. *Historic Structures Report: Fort Vancouver National Historic Site, Washington.* Vol. 1. Denver: National Park Service, U.S. Department of the Interior, 1972.

———. *Historic Structures Report: Fort Vancouver National Historic Site, Washington.* Vol. 2. Denver: National Park Service, U.S. Department of the Interior, 1976.

———. *The History of Fort Vancouver and Its Physical Structure.* Washington State Historical Society and the National Park Service, U.S. Department of Interior. Portland, Ore.: Abbott, Kerns and Bell Co., 1957.

Hymes, James L., Jr. *Care of the Children of Working Mothers.* Interview with Lois Meek Stolz. Carmel, Calif.: Hacienda Press, 1978.

Jackman, S.W., ed. *The Journal of William Sturgis*. Victoria: Sono Nis Press, 1978.

Jenkins, Harold F. *Two Points of View: The History of the Parlor Stereoscope*. Uniontown, Pa: E. G. Warman, 1973.

Jessett, Thomas E., ed. *Reports and Letters of Herbert Beaver, 1836–1838*. Portland, Ore.: Champoeg Press, 1959.

Johansen, Dorothy O., and Charles Gates. *Empire of the Columbia: A History of the Pacific Northwest*. New York: Harper and Row, 1957.

Josephy, Alvin M., Jr. *Chief Joseph's People and Their War*. Yellowstone Association for Natural Science, History and Education, Inc., and the National Park Service, U.S. Department of the Interior, 1964.

———. *The Nez Perce Indians and the Opening of the Northwest*. New Haven, Conn.: Yale University Press, 1965.

Kaiser Company, Inc. *How'dy Stranger*. 1942. Copy at Vancouver National Historic Reserve Trust.

Kaiser Company, Inc. *Ships for Victory*. Portland, Ore.: Glass-Keystone Press, 1944.

Kaiser Company, Inc. *The Ships We Build*. n.d. Copy at Vancouver National Historic Reserve Trust.

The Kaiser Story. Oakland, Calif.: Kaiser Industries Corporation, 1968. Copy at Vancouver National Historic Reserve Trust.

Kammen, Carol, ed. *On Doing Local History: Reflections on What Local Historians Do, Why, and What It Means*. Nashville, Tenn.: American Association for State and Local History, 1986.

———. *The Pursuit of Local History: Readings on Theory and Practice*. Walnut Creek, Calif.: Alta Mira Press, 1996.

Kammen, Michael. *Mystic Chords of Memory: The Transformation of Tradition in American Culture*. New York: Vintage Books, 1993.

Karp, Ivan, Christine Mullens Krammer, and Steven D. Lavine, eds. *Museums and Communities: The Politics of Public Culture*. Washington, D.C.: Smithsonian Institution Press, 1992.

Keyser, James D. *Indian Rock Art of the Columbia Plateau*. Seattle: University of Washington Press, 1992.

Klein, Larry. *Exhibit Planning and Design*. New York: Madison Square Press, 1986.

Koppel, Tom. *Kanaka: The Untold Story of Hawaiian Pioneers in British Columbia and the Pacific Northwest*. Vancouver, British Columbia: Whitecap Books, 1995.

Korff, Ralph, and Betty Korff, comps. *Clark County, Washington, 1880 Census*. Vol. 3. Vancouver, Wash.: Clark County Genealogical Society, 1986.

Kyvig, David E., and Myron A. Marty. *Nearby History: Exploring the Past around You*. Nashville, Tenn.: American Association for State and Local History, 1996.

Lamb, W. Kaye, ed. *The Voyage of George Vancouver, 1791–1795*. London: London's Hakluyt Society, 1984.

Landerholm, Carl. *Vancouver Area Chronology, 1784–1958*. Vancouver, Wash.: City of Vancouver, 1960.

Lang, William L., ed. *A Columbia River Reader*. Vancouver: Washington State Historical Society/Center for Columbia River History, 1992.

Lavender, David, and Archie Satterfield. *Fort Vancouver: Fort Vancouver National Historic Site, Washington*. National Park Handbook Series, no. 113. Washington, D.C.: National Park Service, U.S. Department of the Interior, 1981.

Leckie, William H. *The Buffalo Soldiers: A Narrative of the Negro Cavalry in the West*. Norman: University of Oklahoma Press, 1967.

Lewis, William S., and Naojiro Murakami. *Ranald MacDonald: The Narrative of His Life, 1824–1894*. Portland: Oregon Historical Society Press, 1990.

Lockley, Fred. *History of the Columbia River Valley*. 3 vols. Chicago: S. J. Clarke Publishing Co., 1928.

———. *Oregon Trail Blazers*. New York: Knickerbocker Press, 1929.

Logan, Rayford W. *Howard University: The First Hundred Years, 1867–1967*. New York: New York University Press, 1969.

Loke, Margarett, ed. *The World As It Was, 1865–1921: A Photographic Portrait from the Keystone-Mast Collection*. New York: Summit Books, 1980.

Louis Proctor Air Jubilee. Sunday, 18 August, 1929. Vancouver, Wash. Copy at Vancouver National Historic Reserve Trust.

Lubetkin, Wendy. *George Marshall*. New York: Chelsea House Publishers, 1989.

M. J. Murdock Charitable Trust. *M. J. Murdock Charitable Trust 20th Anniversary Report, 1994 Annual Report*. Vancouver, Wash. Copy at Vancouver National Historic Reserve Trust.

Maben, Manly. *Vanport*. Portland: Oregon Historical Society Press, 1987.

MacColl, E. Kimbark. *Merchants, Money and Power: The Portland Establishment, 1843–1913*. Portland, Ore.: Georgian Press, 1988.

MacKay, Douglas. *The Honorable Company: A History of the Hudson's Bay Company*. Toronto: McClelland and Stewart, 1949.

Major-Frégeau, Madeleine, ed. and intro. *Overland to Oregon in 1845: Impressions of a Journey across North America*. Ottawa: Public Archives of Canada, 1976.

Mares, G. C. *The History of the Typewriter: Successor to the Pen*. Arcadia, Calif.: Post Era Books, 1985.

Marshall, John R. *A History of the Vancouver Public Schools: Vancouver School District No. 37*. Dallas, Tex.: Taylor Publishing, 1975.

McFeely, William S. *Yankee Stepfather: General O.O. Howard and the Freedmen*. New Haven, Conn.: W. W. Norton, 1994.

McWhorter, Lucullus Virgil. *Hear Me, My Chiefs! Nez Perce Legend and History*. Caldwell, Idaho: Caxton Printers, 1952.

———. *Yellow Wolf: His Own Story, 1855–1935*. Caldwell, Idaho: Caxton Printers, 1940.

Merk, Frederick. *Fur Trade and Empire: George Simpson's Journal, 1824–1825*. Cambridge, Mass.: Harvard University Press, 1931.

———. *The Oregon Question: Essays in Anglo-American Diplomacy and Politics*. Cambridge, Mass.: Harvard University Press, 1967.

Merrit, Jane T. *Administrative History, 1993: Fort Vancouver National Historic Site*. Seattle: National Park Service, Department of the Interior, 1993.

Montgomery, Richard G. *The White-Headed Eagle: John McLoughlin, Builder of an Empire*. New York: Macmillan, 1934.

Moolman, Valerie. *Women Aloft*. Alexandria, Va.: Time-Life, 1981.

Morse, S. L. *Household Discoveries and Mrs. Curtis's Cookbook*. New York: Success Company, 1908.

Newhall, Beaumont. *The History of Photography*. New York: Museum of Modern Art, 1964.

Newman, Peter C. *Empire of the Bay: An Illustrated History of the Hudson's Bay Company*. Toronto: Madison Press, 1989.

Nicandri, David. *Northwest Chiefs: Gustav Sohon's Views of the 1855 Stevens Treaty Councils*. Tacoma: Washington State Historical Society, 1986.

The 1932 Year Book. Clark County *Sun*. Vancouver, Wash. Copy at Vancouver National Historic Reserve Trust.

Nisbet, Jack. *Sources of the River: Tracking David Thompson across Western North America*. Seattle: Sasquatch Books, 1994.

O'Donnell, Terence. *An Arrow in the Earth: General Joel Palmer and the Indians of Oregon*. Portland: Oregon Historical Society Press, 1991.

Official Annual 1937: Vancouver Barracks, Civilian Conservation Corps, Ninth Corps Area, 1938. Copy at Vancouver National Historic Reserve Trust.

Official Programme: Vancouver, Clarke County, USA, 4 July 1909. Copy at Vancouver National Historic Reserve Trust.

O'Meara, Walter. *Daughters of the Country: The Women of the Fur Traders and Mountain Men*. New York: Harcourt, Brace and World, 1968.

The Oregonian Souvenir: Portland, Oregon, 1850–1892. Portland, Ore.: Lewis & Dryden, 1892.

O'Sullivan, Thomas J., and Karl B. Weber. *History of the United States Pioneer and Government Operated Air Mail Service, 1910–1928*. Philadelphia: American Air Mail Society, 1973.

Parrish, Thomas. *Roosevelt and Marshall, Partners in Politics and War: The Personal Story*. New York: William Morrow, 1989.

Perkins, Norris H. *Slow Settles the Dust in Oregon*. Portland, Ore.: Four Mountain Productions, 1991.

Peters, Harry T. *Currier & Ives: Printmakers to the American People*. New York: Doubleday, Doran & Co., 1942.

Petersen, Henry C. *The Centralia Horror: Up and in Action*. Seattle: Washington Branch General Defense Committee, 1919.

Pictorial Gallery of Arts, Useful Arts. London: Charles Knight and Co., n.d.

Plummer, Katherine. *The Shogun's Reluctant Ambassadors: Japanese Sea Drifters in the North Pacific*. Portland: Oregon Historical Society Press, 1991.

Prentiss, A. M. *Pictorial Review of World's War Activities: Spruce Production Division, U.S. Army, Oregon and Washington*. Portland, Ore.: A. M. Prentiss, 1918.

Preuss, Charles. *Exploring with Fremont*. Norman: University of Oklahoma Press, 1958.

Ramsey, Jarold, ed. *Coyote Was Going There: Indian Literature of the Oregon Country*. Seattle: University of Washington Press, 1977.

Ray, Verne F. *Lower Chinook Ethnographic Notes*. Vol. 7. University of Washington Publications in Anthropology. Seattle: University of Washington Press, 1938.

Reed, Walt. *John Clymer: An Artist's Rendezvous with the Frontier West*. Flagstaff, Ariz.: Northland Press, 1976.

Rehr, Darryl. *Antique Typewriters and Office Collectibles Identification and Value Guide*. Paducah, Ky.: Schroeder Publishing Co., 1997.

Reps, John W. *Panoramas of Promise: Pacific Northwest Cities and Towns on Nineteenth-Century Lithographs*. Pullman, Wash.: Washington State University Press, 1984.

Rich, E.E., ed. *The Letters of John McLoughlin from Fort Vancouver to the Governor and Committee, First Series, 1825–38*. Hudson's Bay Company Series. Vol. 4. Toronto: Champlain Society, 1941.

———. *The Letters of John McLoughlin from Fort Vancouver to the Governor and Committee, Second Series, 1839–44*. Hudson's Bay Company Series. Vol. 6. Toronto: Champlain Society, 1943.

———. *The Letters of John McLoughlin from Fort Vancouver to the Governor and Committee, Third Series, 1844–46*. Hudson's Bay Company Series. Vol. 7. Toronto: Champlain Society, 1944.

Rigdon, Paul. *Captain Robert Gray's Chart Discovered after Almost Two Centuries*. Spokane, Wash.: Gonzaga University Press, 1976.

Rose, Mary Kline. *The Celebrate Freedom Publication Series*. 5 vols. Vancouver, Wash.: Heritage Trust of Clark County, 1991.

———. *The Medal of Honor and Department of Columbia*. Vol. 3. Vancouver, Wash.: Heritage Trust of Clark County, 1991.

Ross, Alexander. *Adventures of the First Settlers on the Oregon or Columbia River . . . of the Pacific*. Ed. by James P. Ronda. 1849 text. Lincoln: University of Nebraska Press, 1986.

———. *The Fur Hunters of the Far West*. Ed. by Kenneth A. Spaulding. 1855 text. Norman: University of Oklahoma Press, 1956.

Ross, Lester A. *Fort Vancouver, 1829–1860: A Historical Archaeological Investigation of the Goods Imported and Manufactured by the Hudson's Bay Company*. Seattle: National Park Service, 1992.

Ruby, Robert H., and John A. Brown. *The Chinook Indians: Traders of the Lower Columbia River*. Norman: University of Oklahoma Press, 1976.

Schlick, Mary Dodds. *Columbia River Basketry: Gift of the Ancestors, Gift of the Earth*. Seattle: University of Washington Press, 1994.

Schoenberg, Wilfred P. *A History of the Catholic Church in the Pacific Northwest, 1743–1983*. Washington, D.C.: Pastoral Press, 1987.

Schwantes, Carlos A. *The Pacific Northwest: An Interpretive History*. Lincoln: University of Nebraska Press, 1989.

Scofield, John. *Hail Columbia: Robert Gray, John Kendrick and the Pacific Fur Trade*. Portland: Oregon Historical Society Press, 1993.

Settle, Raymond W., ed. *The March of the Mounted Riflemen: . . . May to October, 1849, as Recorded in the Journals of Major Osborne Cross and George Gibbs and the Official Report of Colonel Loring*. Reprint. Glendale, Calif.: Arthur H. Clark, 1940.

Seventh U.S. Infantry Yearbook, 1929. Vancouver Barracks, Washington. Copy at Vancouver National Historic Reserve Trust.

Sheppe, Walter, ed. *Journal of the Voyage to the Pacific: Alexander MacKenzie*. New York: Dover Publications, 1995.

Sherman, Edgar. *The Seventeenth: The Squadron with a Reputation*. Portland, Ore.: Boyer Printing Company, 1918.

Sims, Edward H. *Aces Talk*. New York: Ballantine Books, 1972.

Skinner, Constance L. *Adventures of Oregon: A Chronicle of the Fur Trade*. New Haven, Conn.: Yale University Press, 1921.

Smith, Sherry L. *The View from Officer's Row: Army Perceptions of Western Indians*. Tucson: University of Arizona Press, 1990.

Sorley, L. S. *History of the Fourteenth United States Infantry*. Chicago: privately printed, 1909.

Staff, Frank. *The Picture Postcard and Its Origins*. New York: Frederick A. Praeger, Inc. 1966.

Stanley, George F. G., ed. *Mapping the Frontier: Charles Wilson's Diary of the Survey of the 49th Parallel, 1858–1862*. Seattle: University of Washington Press, 1970.

Stenzel, Franz. *James Madison Alden: Yankee Artist of the Pacific Coast, 1854–1860*. Fort Worth, Tex.: Amon Carter Museum, 1975.

———. *The Drawings of James G. Swan: Early Days in the Northwest*. Portland, Ore.: Portland Art Museum, 1959.

Stewart, Hilary. *The Adventures and Sufferings of John R. Jewitt, Captive of Maquinna*. Toronto: Douglas and McIntyre, 1987.

The Story of the 91st Division, San Francisco. San Mateo, Calif.: 91st Division Publication Committee, 1919. Copy at Vancouver National Historic Reserve Trust.

Strickler, Carol. *American Woven Coverlets*. Loveland, Colo.: Interweave Press, 1987.

Sturtevant, William C., and Wayne P. Suttles, eds. *Handbook of North American Indians: Northwest Coast*. Vol. 7. Washington, D.C.: Smithsonian Institution, 1990.

Sully, Langdon. *No Tears for the General: The Life of Alfred Sully, 1821–1879*. Palo Alto, Calif.: American West Publishing Company, 1974.

Swan, James G. *The Northwest Coast*. 1857 text. Reprint. Fairfield, Wash.: Ye Galleon Press, 1966.

Taylor, Albert P., and Ralph S. Kuykendall, eds. *The Hawaiian Islands, Early Relations with the Pacific Northwest*. Papers read during the Captain Cook Sesquicentennial Celebration, Honolulu, 17 August, 1928. Honolulu: Captain Cook Sesquicentennial Commission and the Archives of Hawaii Commission, 1930.

Turner, Lucien M. *Ethnology of the Ungava District, Hudson Bay Territory*. Washington, D.C.: Smithsonian Institution, 1894.

Van Arsdol, Ted. *Northwest Bastion: The U.S. Army Barracks at Vancouver, 1849–1916*. Vancouver, Wash.: Heritage Trust of Clark County, 1991.

———. *Vancouver on the Columbia: An Illustrated History*. Woodbridge, Calif: Windsor Publications, 1986.

Van Kirk, Sylvia. *Many Tender Ties: Women in Fur-Trade Society, 1670–1870*. Norman: University of Oklahoma Press, 1980.

Van der Linden, F. Robert. *The Boeing 247: The First Modern Airliner*. Seattle: University of Washington Press, 1998.

Vancouver Historical Study Commission. *Final Report: Vancouver National Historical Reserve Feasibility Study and Environmental Assessment*. Vancouver, Wash.: 1993.

Vancouver Housing Authority. *50 Years of Progress Dedicated to People*. Vancouver Housing Authority, 1993. Copy at Vancouver National Historic Reserve Trust.

Vancouver Housing Authority. *A Tale of Six Cities and How They Became a Permanent Part of Vancouver, Washington*. n.d. Copy at Vancouver National Historic Reserve Trust.

Vaughan, Thomas, ed. *The Western Shore: Oregon Country Essays Honoring the American Revolution*. Portland: Oregon Historical Society Press, 1975.

Vaughan, Thomas, and A.A. St. C.M. Murray-Oliver. *Captain Cook, R.N., the Resolute Mariner: An International Record of Oceanic Discovery*. Portland: Oregon Historical Society Press, 1974.

Viola, Herman J. *Magnificent Voyagers: The U.S. Exploring Expedition, 1838–1842*. Washington, D.C.: Smithsonian Institution, 1985.

Walker, Jon. *A Century Airborne: Air Trails of Pearson Airpark*. Vancouver, Wash.: Rose Wind Press, 1994.

Warre, Henry J. *Sketches in North America and the Oregon Territory*. 1848. Reprint. Barre, Mass.: Imprint Society, 1970.

Warren, Robert Penn. *Chief Joseph of the Nez Perce: A Poem by Robert Penn Warren*. New York: Random House, 1982.

Waterloo, Stanley, ed. *Our Living Leaders*. Chicago: Monarch Book Company, n.d.

Watkins, Carleton E. *Photographs of the Columbia River and Oregon*. Ed. by David Featherstone. Carmel, Calif.: Friends of Photography, 1979.

———. *Photographs from the J. Paul Getty Museum*. Ed. by Weston Naef. Los Angeles: J. Paul Getty Museum, 1997.

White, Richard. *The Organic Machine*. New York: Hill and Wang, 1995.

Wilkes, Charles. *Narrative of the United States Exploring Expedition during the Years 1838, 1839, 1840, 1841, 1842*. 5 vols. Philadelphia: Lee & Blanchard, 1845.

Wing, Paul. *Stereoscopes: The First One Hundred Years*. Nashua, N.H.: Transition Publishing, 1996.

Wolfe, Cheri. *Lt. Charles Wilkes and the Great U.S. Exploring Expedition*. New York: Chelsea House Publishers, 1991.

Wood, Erskine. *Days with Chief Joseph*. Vancouver, Wash.: Rose Wind Press, 1991.

Xydes, Georgia. *Alexander MacKenzie and the Explorers of Canada*. New York: Chelsea House Publishers, 1992.

II. ARTICLES, NEWSPAPERS, PERIODICALS

Anderson, Thomas M. "Aguinaldo's True Report of the Philippine Insurrection." *Journal of the Military Service Institution of the United States* 57, 196 (July–August 1915): 3–10.

———. "Vancouver Barracks and the Mission of St. James." *West Shore* (August 1883): 307–14.

———. "Vancouver, the Oldest Town in Washington Territory." *West Shore* (August 1883): 189–90.

———. "The Vancouver Reservation Case: A Legal Romance." *Oregon Historical Quarterly* 8 (December 1907): 219–30.

Andreyev, Igor. "The Plane That Joined Two Continents." *Soviet Life* (July 1987): 35.

Barry, J. Neilson. "Broughton, up Columbia River 1792." *Oregon Historical Quarterly* 32 (December 1931): 301–12.

———. "Columbia River Exploration, 1792." Parts 1, 2. *Oregon Historical Quarterly* 33 (March, June 1932): 31–42, 143–55.

Bingham, Kate Stevens. "The Spirit of '76: A Visit to Vancouver Barracks." *Clark County History* (1966): 138–41.

Blue, George Verne. "Green's Missionary Report on Oregon, 1829." *Oregon Historical Quarterly* 30 (September 1929): 259–71.

———. "A Hudson's Bay Company Contract for Hawaiian Labor." *Oregon Historical Quarterly* 25 (March 1924): 72–75.

Bona, Milton. "David Douglas at Vancouver." *Clark County History* 16 (1975): 87–99.

———. "Hawaiians Made Life 'More Bearable' at Fort Vancouver." *Clark County History* 13 (1972): 158–75.

———. "The Truth about U. S. Grant at Vancouver." *Clark County History* 15 (1974): 421–39.

Bo's'n's Whistle. 1941–1945. Biweekly employee magazine for the Oregon Shipbuilding Corporation of Portland and Kaiser Companies, Inc., Vancouver and Swan Island.

Bullard, Oral. "Why Not a Marker for the Civilian Conservation Corps?" *Northwest Magazine* (12 November 1972): 10.

Burke, Kathleen. "Together We Win! Get a War Job! Save Waste Fats!" *Smithsonian* 24 (March 1994): 66–69.

Cairns, Arline Anderson. "The Gay Nineties in Vancouver." *Clark County History* (1961): 31–41.

Canon, Belle. "The Kaiser Shipyard Experiment of WW II: A Forgotten Revolution in Child Care." *Oregon Times Magazine* (February-March 1976): 21–24.

Carriker, Robert C. "The Seven-Fanged Horror of the Pacific: Father Peter DeSmet Crosses the Columbia Bar." *Columbia* (Winter 1995/96): 34–37.

Caughlin, Judy. "Headline 1933: Drastic Changes Planned, Senate OK's Forest Camps." *Clark County History* (1983): 32–37.

Challenger. Vancouver Barracks. Vol. 1, no.1 (July 1943)–vol. 3, no. 26 (7 February 1946).

Clancy, Kathleen. "The Army Post Town." *Clark County History* 2 (1961): 95–99.

Clark County Register (Clark County, Wash.). 11 July 1863; 18 July 1863; 6 January 1887; 4 January 1893.

Clark, Donald H. "Sawmill on the Columbia." *Beaver* (June 1950): 42–44.

Clark, Robert Carlton. "Hawaiians in Early Oregon." *Oregon Historical Quarterly* (1943): 21–31.

Coffin, Howard. "Soldier, Statesman, Scholar: The Remarkable Life of Gen. O. O. Howard." *Vermont Sunday Magazine* (1 May 1988): 4–5, 14–15.

Collier's: The National Weekly. 1914–1918. New York: P. F. Collier and Son.

Columbian (Vancouver, Wash.). Years consulted: 1942, 1943, 1946, 1986.

Elliott, T. C. "British Values in Oregon, 1847." *Oregon Historical Quarterly* 32 (March 1931): 27–45.

———. "The Northern Boundary of Oregon." *Oregon Historical Quarterly* 20 (March 1919): 25–34.

———. "The Northwest Boundaries." *Oregon Historical Quarterly* 20 (December 1919): 331–44.

Emmons, George Thorton, ed. "Extracts from the Emmons Journal." *Oregon Historical Quarterly* 26 (September 1925): 263–73.

Frost, Jess. "From Moscow to America over the North Pole: A Bridge To Be Used." *Soviet Life* (June 1984): 8–9, 14.

Fry, Ken. "Vancouver's Boom Town War Years." *Clark County History* 28 (1987): 45–54.

Gauld, Charles A. "Thomas M. Anderson: First U.S. General Overseas." *Clark County History* (1973): 248–69.

Glover, R. "York Boats." *Beaver* (March 1949): 20–23.

"Great Spruce Cut-up Plant Starts Operations." *Timberman* (February 1918): 35.

Harper's Weekly. 27 (October, November 1877). New York.

Hawking, Richard. "In Commemoration, George C. Marshall." *Clark County History* 21 (1980): 73–74.

Hirtzel, Robert L. "The Covington Piano." *Clark County History* 8 (1967): 204.

———. "Music of Voyageurs, and a Scot." *Clark County History* 1 (1960): 33–36.

Howay, F. W., and T. C. Elliott. "Vancouver's Brig *Chatham* in the Columbia." *Oregon Historical Quarterly* 43 (December 1944): 318–27.

Hussey, John A. "The Women of Fort Vancouver." *Oregon Historical Quarterly* 92 (Fall 1991): 265–308.

"I Was a 'Hello Girl'." *Yankee.* (March 1979): 67–71, 102–06.

Iverson, Lance. "The History and Significance of Vancouver Barracks and Officers Row." *Clark County History* 29 (1988): 61–69.

Jones, Roy F. "Clark County Aviation." *Clark County History* (1968): 299–323.

Klan, Yvonne Mearns. "Kanaka William." *Beaver* (Spring 1979): 38–43.

Knuth, Priscilla, ed., "HMS *Modeste* on the Pacific Coast, 1843–47: Log and Letters." *Oregon Historical Quarterly* 61 (December 1960): 408–36.

Landerholm, Carl. "The Covingtons and Covington House." *Clark County History* 1 (1960): 5–9.

Leader, Herman A. "McLoughlin's Answer to Warre Report." *Oregon Historical Quarterly* 33 (September 1932): 214–29.

Lomax, Alfred L. "Hawaii-Columbia River Trade in Early Days." *Oregon Historical Quarterly* 43 (December 1942): 328–38.

Minto, John. "Reminiscences of Experiences on the Oregon Trail in 1844." *Oregon Historical Quarterly* 2 (September 1901): 209–54.

Morning Oregonian (Portland). 12 June 1912.

Oregon Spectator (Oregon City). 5 February 1846–20 January 1848.

Oregonian (Portland). 21–22 June 1937; 16 July 1937; 15 July 1993; 29 December 1994; 2 June 1997; 13 June 1997; 8 March 1998; 24 May 1998, 28 June 1998.

"Pacific-Northwest Army Flier Ordered to New Post." *Pacific Airport News* (February 1928): 19.

The Penny Magazine of the Society for the Diffusion of Useful Knowledge 4 (1835). London: Charles Knight and Co.

Peterson, Keith. "George C. Marshall at Vancouver: Preface to an Heroic Career." *Clark County History* 14 (1976): 21–43.

Pollard, Royce E. "The Presence and Missions of the United States Army at Vancouver Barracks, Vancouver, Wash., 1849–1898." *Clark County History* 30 (1988): 31–39.

Powell, Fred Wilbur. "Hall Jackson Kelley, Prophet of Oregon." *Oregon Historical Quarterly* 18 (March 1917): 1–53; (June 1917): 93–139; (Sept. 1917): 167–224.

Rankin, J. G. "Aviation in Pacific Northwest." *Pacific Airport News* (February 1928).

Ransom, Victoria L. "Officers Row at Vancouver Barracks." *Clark County History* (1962): 38–41.

"Representing Native American History." *Public Historian: A Journal of Public History* 18 (Fall 1996).

Ronda, James P. "The Education of an Empire Builder: John Jacob Astor and the World of the Columbia." *Columbia* (Fall 1997): 18–23.

Ross, Lester A. "Trade Beads from Hudson's Bay Company Fort Vancouver, 1829–1860." *Beads-Annual Journal* (1991).

Salnikov, Yuri. "The Chkalov Committee, Our Friends in Vancouver." *Soviet Life* (August 1979): 30–31.

———. "Handshake across the Arctic Ocean." *Soviet Life* (July 1987): 28–30, 46–49.

Sandwich Island Gazette (Honolulu). 13 May 1837.

Sandwich Island News (Honolulu). 20 January 1847.

Schafer, Joseph, ed. "Documents Relative to Warre and Vavasour's Military Reconnaissance in Oregon 1845–6." *Oregon Historical Quarterly* 10 (March 1909): 1–99.

Scott, Leslie M. "Influence of American Settlement upon the Oregon Boundary Treaty of 1846." *Oregon Historical Quarterly* 29 (March 1928): 1–19.

Shippee, Lester Burrell. "The Federal Relations of Oregon." *Oregon Historical Quarterly* 20 (March, June, September, December 1919): 35–93, 173–218, 261–95, 345–95.

Slacum, William A. "Slacum's Report on Oregon, 1836–37." *Oregon Historical Quarterly* 13 (June 1912): 175–224.

Smith, Cherry L. "Reimagining the Indian: Charles Eskine Scott Wood and Frank Linderman." *Pacific Northwest Quarterly* 87 (Summer 1996): 149–58.

Spitzer, Paul. "When Russians Landed in Vancouver." *Columbia* (Summer 1987): 5–12.

The Sport. (23 November 1896).

Stevens, Mark. "Chief Joseph's Revenge." *New Yorker* (October 1995): 26–33.

Straight Grain. Vancouver Barracks. 26 October 1918– 21 December 1918.

Strelnikov, Boris. "Vancouver Salutes Pioneer Soviet Aviators." *Soviet Life* (September 1975): 30–31.

Swanson, Bob. "What Happened to the Spruce Camps?" *La Posta: A Journal of American Postal History* (September 1992): 50–54.

Taylor, Teresa. "Fort Vancouver Fourth of July Celebration." *Clark County History* 29 (1988): 91–100.

The Timberman (Portland). 19 (April, September 1918).

Times (London). June 1835.

Tsyganov, Igor. "Valeri Chkalov." *Soviet Life* (July 1987): 36–39.

Turnbull, Elsie. "Fort Shepherd." *Beaver* (Autumn 1959): 42–47.

Van Arsdol, Ted. "The Famed Fourteenth: Vancouver's Favorite, 1865– 1886, 1884–1893." *Clark County History* 12 (1971): 73–101.

———. "The Famed Fourteenth: Vancouver's Favorite, 1893–1917." *Clark County History* 13 (1972): 191–226.

———. "World War II in Vancouver." *Clark County History* 19 (1978): 5–32.

Vancouver Chronicle (Wash.). 6 June 1861.

Vancouver Daily Columbian (Wash.). "Military Personals." (8 January 1892); other years consulted: 1893, 1918, 1919.

Vancouver Evening Columbian (Wash.). Years consulted: 1920, 1924, 1925.

Vancouver Independent (Wash.). Years and columns consulted: 1876; 1877 "Post Items"; 1878 "Local"; 1879–80 "Military Items"; 1886 "Military and Personal"; 1889.

"War Housing." *Architectural Forum* 76 (May 1942).

White, Lily E. "From the Log of the *Raysark*." *Pacific Monthly* 16 (August 1906): 160–65.

Zinsser, Caroline. "The Best Day Care There Ever Was." *Working Mother* (October 1984): 76–80.

III. Unpublished Theses, Papers, Musical Scores, Manuscripts

Anderson, Arline. "A Daughter of Uncle Sam: Reminiscences of Arline Anderson Cairns, 1869–1932." Copy at Clark County Museum, Vancouver, Wash.

Battle, Thomas C. "Oliver Otis Howard: A Man for His Times." Paper presented at Washington State University, Vancouver. November 1994.

Borun, Minda. "Measuring the Immeasurable: A Pilot Study of Museum Effectiveness." Conducted at the Franklin Institute Science Museum and Planetarium, 1977.

"Cannon, William, 1755–1854." Biographical information presented at St. Paul, Oregon, cemetery ceremony, 1991. Copy at Clark County Museum, Vancouver, Wash.

Chief Joseph to General O. O. Howard. Oakland Agency, Indian Territory, 30 June 1880. Correspondence. Copy at Vancouver National Historic Reserve Trust.

Civilian Conservation Corps. Ninth Corps Area newsletters: Vancouver Barracks *Review,* the *Penguin, Tower Rock Sentinel,* and *Yellow Jacket.* Washington State Historical Society, Special Collections.

CCC Archives. U.S. Forest Service, Pacific Northwest Region, Portland, Ore.

Clark, Erma Fordyce. "History of Vancouver Barracks." Vancouver Barracks Historical Files. Headquarters, Vancouver Barracks, n.d. Copy at Vancouver National Historic Reserve Trust.

Columbia Rediviva Papers, 1785–1852. MSS 957. Oregon Historical Society, Portland.

Columbia River Bicentennial Commission, State of Oregon. "This Noble River," "Adventure and Encounter," "Exploration and Encounter." Files. Vancouver National Historic Reserve Trust.

Corbett, Henry Winslow. Correspondence, 1937–1944. MSS 1110. Oregon Historical Society, Portland.

Correspondence between Gen. Henry C. Hodges, Buffalo, New York, and Major Boutelle, regarding early history of Vancouver Barracks and McClellan's expedition. 17 November 1905. Copy at Vancouver National Historic Reserve Trust.

Daily remarks on board HMS *Modeste* while moored off Fort Vancouver, 29 November 1845–3 May 1847. Copy at Fort Vancouver National Historic Site, from originals at Public Record Office, London. Record no. ADM 53/2815.

Dale Denny Collection. Clippings file, *Oregon Journal.* Photographs from 1930s. Vancouver National Historic Reserve Trust.

Delgado, James P. "Continuity, Conflict and Change: The Hudson's Bay Company on the Northwest Coast, 1824–1861." Exhibit text. Vancouver Maritime Museum, Vancouver, British Columbia, 1995.

———. "Maritime Activities of the Hudson's Bay Company." Paper presented at Fort Vancouver National Historic Site in honor of the fiftieth anniversary of the establishment of the fort, 17 July 1998.

———. "Shipbuilding, Boat Building and Repair at Fort Vancouver, 1825–1846: A Historical and Archaeological Perspective." Vancouver Maritime Museum, Vancouver, British Columbia, n.d.

"Echoes of Oregon, 1837–1859: A Selection of Records from the Oregon State Archives." Oregon State Archives, Office of the Secretary of State, Salem, 1987.

Employees' private letters, undelivered, 1775–1871. Hudson's Bay Company Archives, Provincial Archives of Manitoba, Winnipeg.

Farr, Maj. William. "The Stockaders" Scrapbook. Vancouver Cenaqua Pageant, 1950. Copy at Vancouver National Historic Reserve Trust.

Gauld, Charles Anderson. "Gen. T. M. Anderson in the Philippines, 1898–1899, or Grandpa Captured Manila." New York City. July 1944. Copy at Vancouver National Historic Reserve Trust.

Gibson, Kenneth. "My Discovery of Historical Fort Defiance 'Winter Quarters' of Captain Robert Gray, 1791–92." Tofino, British Columbia. Copy at Vancouver National Historic Reserve Trust, n.d.

Hansen, David. "The Hudson Bay Company and the Whitman Murders of 1847." Copy at Fort Vancouver National Historic Site, n.d.

Hardesty, Von. "Historical Overview of Pearson Airfield." Paper submitted to the National Park Service, Pacific Northwest Region, Seattle, 1992.

Hayden, Mary Jane. Journal, 1850. MSS 1508. Oregon Historical Society, Portland.

Hill, Sarah. Diary, 1843. MSS 1508. Oregon Historical Society, Portland.

Howard, H. S. Paper presented at Howard University. Charter Day, c. 1920. Copy at Vancouver National Historic Reserve Trust.

Kaiser Permanente. Historical files. Portland, Ore.

Kardas, Susan. "The People Bought This and the Clatsop Became Rich: A View of Nineteenth-Century Fur Trade Relationships on the Lower Columbia between Chinookan Speakers, Whites and Kanakas." Ph.D. diss., Bryn Mawr College, Penn. 1971.

Landerholm, Carl. "The Genesis of Apple Culture in Washington and the Pacific Northwest." Fort Vancouver Historical Society, 1952. Copy at Vancouver National Historic Reserve Trust.

———. "Vancouver Area Chronology, 1784–1958." Vancouver, Wash., 1960. Copy at Vancouver National Historic Reserve Trust.

Landstorm, Karl S. Correspondence with city of Vancouver public information office regarding Civilian Conservation Corps at Vancouver Barracks. 15 April 1997.

Leverett Richards Papers. Clippings file on aviation history, *Oregonian,* 1930–1947. Copies at Vancouver National Historic Reserve Trust.

Louis Lee Collection. Kaiser shipyard. Vancouver National Historic Reserve Trust.

Lowe, Thomas. "Private Journal Kept at Fort Vancouver, Columbia River, 1843–1846." Copy at Fort Vancouver National Historic Site.

Loyal Legion of Loggers and Lumbermen. Convention Minutes. 4 March 1918, 5 August 1918.

McGeorge, Maj. Stephen C., USA (retired). Correspondence with author, November 1998. Vancouver National Historic Reserve Trust.

McLellan, Sister Mary DeSales. "Vancouver, Washington, 1846 to 1870, with an Introduction Covering the Hudson's Bay Period." Master's thesis, University of Oregon, 1935.

National Register of Historic Places. Inventory nomination form. Officers Row Historic District, 1974. Copy at Vancouver National Historic Reserve Trust.

National Register of Historic Places. Inventory nomination form for federal properties. Vancouver Barracks, 1984. Copy at Vancouver National Historic Reserve Trust.

Naughton, E. Momilani. "Hawaiians in the Fur Trade: Cultural Influence on the Northwest Coast, 1811–1875." Master's thesis, Western Washington University, 1983.

Nichols, Capt. Frederic C. Correspondence. War Department, Adjutant General's Office, Washington, D.C., 20 February 1880. Clark County Museum, Vancouver, Wash.

Norris Perkins Collection. Howard family papers, photographs. Copies at Vancouver National Historic Reserve Trust.

North American Boundary Commission. "List of Photographs Taken in the Years 1860, 1861." Royal Engineers Library, Brompton Barracks, Kent, England. Copy at Vancouver National Historic Reserve Trust.

Ostermiller, Jerry. "Reconnaissance Survey Report on the Shipwreck *Isabella.*" Columbia River Maritime Museum, Astoria, Ore. 29 June 1994.

Relaford, Judith. "When the Northwest Was Pacific: Gen. O.O. Howard at Home in Portland, 1874–1877." Unpublished paper at Oregon Historical Society, Portland.

Robeson, Robert L. Correspondence with the city of Vancouver. National Association of Civilian Conservation Corps Alumni, Northwest Region, Seattle, Wash., 1997.

Rodgers, Michael W. Correspondence with author. Signal Corps Museum, Fort Gordon, Georgia. 4 October 1996.

Sanborn Insurance Maps of Vancouver, Clarke Co., Washington. 1907, 1911, 1928, 1948, 1951. Clark County Museum.

Schimmel, Julie. "John Mix Stanley and Imagery of the West in Nineteenth-Century American Art." Ph.D. diss., New York University, 1983.

Selby, Jennie Rose Young. Personal correspondence from France, 1917–1919. Copy at Vancouver National Historic Reserve Trust.

Spalding, Eliza. Diary, 1836. MSS 1201. Oregon Historical Society, Portland.

Stark, Robert, and Tim Coulter. "Furnishing Plan for the Chief Factor's House." 1976. Typescript at Fort Vancouver National Historic Site.

Throop, Elizabeth Gail. "Utterly Visionary and Chimerical: A Federal Response to the Depression, and Examination of Civilian Conservation Corps Construction on National Forest System Lands in the Pacific Northwest." Master's thesis, Portland State University, 1979.

Van Arsdol, Ted. Interview with Col. George VanWay. 14 September 1990. Copy at Vancouver National Historic Reserve Trust.

Wagner, Jim. "In Memory of Ordnance Sergeant Moses William." 1991. Copy at Vancouver National Historic Reserve Trust.

———. "In Memory of Private Herman Pfisterer." 1991. Copy at Vancouver National Historic Reserve Trust.

Washington State Department of Transportation, Southwest Region. Historical files.

IV. PUBLIC DOCUMENTS

Davis, Jefferson. *Report to the Assistant Adjutant General's Office, Military Division of the Pacific, 1872.* Copy at Vancouver National Historic Reserve Trust.

National Archives. Fort Vancouver, Wash. Miscellaneous maps and plans, RG 94.

National Archives. Office of the Chief of Engineers. Fort Vancouver, Wash. Territory. Miscellaneous forts file, commanding officers, RG 77.

National Archives. Office of the Quartermaster General. Vancouver Barracks, Wash. Blueprint file, RG 92.

U.S. Congress. House. *Charges Against General Howard.* 41ST Congress, 2nd sess. Report no. 121.

U.S. Congress. House. *Claims of Nez Perce Indians for Compensation for Services Claimed to Have Been Rendered . . . under General O. O. Howard, U.S.A., during the War with Joseph's Band of Nez Perces in 1877.* 56th Congress, 1st sess. U.S. Interior Department, Office of Indian Affairs. Document no. 552.

U.S. Congress. Senate. *Message from the President of the United States, Communicating in Answer to a Senate Resolution of November 13, 1877, Information in Relation to the Cause and Probable Cost of the Late Nez Perces War.* 45th Congress, 2nd sess. Senate Exec. Doc. no. 14.

U.S. Department of Defense. Quartermaster plan files, 1905–1936, Vancouver Barracks, Wash.

V. Sound and Video Recordings, Internet Sources

Aust, Carroll. Interview with author. 29 May 1997. "Marshall Memories." Vancouver, Wash., Clark/Vancouver Television. Videocassette.

Baidukov, Georgiy. Interview on Soviet TV. 1987. Moscow. Videocassette.

Bell, Geraldine. Interview with author. 28 May 1997. Vancouver, Wash., Clark/Vancouver Television. Videocassette.

Castrey, Warren. Interview with author. 10 June 1998. Hockinson, Wash., Vancouver National Historic Reserve Trust. Audiocassette.

Caughlin, Judy. Twenty-six oral history interviews with former Civilian Conservation Corps workers. 1992. History files, Gifford Pinchot National Forest, Wash. Audiocassettes.

"The CCC Contribution on the Columbia." Fort Vancouver Historical Society of Clark County. 1983. Videocassette.

Delgado, James. Telephone interview with author. 1 September 1998. Vancouver, Wash.

Denny, Dale. Interview with author. 3, 27 March 1998. Vancouver, Wash., Vancouver National Historic Reserve Trust. Audiocassette.

Farr, Bill. Telephone interview with author. 3 March 1998. Vancouver, Wash.

"Kalapuya Love Song." Recorded by Leo T. Frachtenberg. Federal Cylinder Project. Wax cylinder.

Moore, Bill. Interview with author. 5 May 1995. Portland, Ore. Audiocassette.

Morrison, Pearl. Interview with author. 10 February 1998. Vancouver, Wash., Vancouver National Historic Reserve Trust. Audiocassette.

Nez Perce Music Archive. "Chief Joseph and Stephen Reuben." Recorded by Alice C. Fletcher. 6 April 1900. Archive of Folksong (American Folklife Center). Library of Congress, Washington, D.C. Wax cylinder.

O'Donnell, Victoria. "Women, War and Work." KUSM-TV Montana Public Television. 1994. Videocassette.

Paddock, Hudson. Interview with author. 13 May 1997, 6 January 1998. Vancouver, Wash.

Pistolhead, Elsie. Recorded by Eugene Hunn. 15 December 1976. Special Collections, University of Washington, Seattle. Audiocassette.

Scott, Vivian. Telephone interview with author. 11 February 1998. Vancouver, Wash.

Singer, Amy. Interview with author. 26 February 1998. Vancouver, Wash.

Songs of the Voyageurs. 1998. St. Paul: Minnesota Historical Society Press. Compact disc.

Stanek, Caroline. Interview with author. 18 March 1998. Vancouver, Wash., Vancouver National Historic Reserve Trust. Audiocassette.

Taps Story. http://www.iinet.net.au/~oneil/scouts/songs/tapstory.

United States Military Academy Band. *Heritage of the March.* "Howard March," published in 1903 by Wurlitzer; "General Miles," published in 1896 by Coleman. Stereo record.

Unter dem Sternenbanner Militär Marsch. Verlag and Eigenthum von Karl Hochstein Gustav Mueller, Heidelberg, n.d.

VanWay, Col. George I., USA. Correspondence and telephone interviews with author. December 1995–July 1996, Vancouver, Wash.

INDEX

COLOPHON

The content of this book is based on the exhibit "One Place across Time," located in the O.O. Howard House on the Vancouver National Historic Reserve in Vancouver, Washington.

Book Design:
Larry Rank, Vancouver National Historic Reserve Trust

Typeface:
ITC Giovanni
The typeface was designed by Robert Slimbach in 1989 and is based on such classic faces as Garamond and Bembo, but features more contemporary proportions and weights.

Hardware:
Computers: Apple Macintosh PowerBook 3400/200 and G4/400
Scanners: Umax 2400S, Microtek 6400

Software:
Layouts and index: Adobe PageMaker, BBEdit
Photographs: Adobe Photoshop
Illustrations: Adobe Illustrator, Fractal Design Painter

Paper:
70# Cougar Opaque, smooth, white

Printing:
Publishers Press, Salt Lake City, Utah

To hear the exhibit's audio components, visit our website at http://VancouverHistoricReserveTrust.org